Anonymous

An authentic Account of the Debates in the House of Lords

On Tuesday, December 9, Monday, December 15, and Wednesday, December 17,

1783, on the Bill

Anonymous

An authentic Account of the Debates in the House of Lords
On Tuesday, December 9, Monday, December 15, and Wednesday, December 17, 1783, on the Bill

ISBN/EAN: 9783337151959

Printed in Europe, USA, Canada, Australia, Japan

Cover: Foto ©ninafisch / pixelio.de

More available books at **www.hansebooks.com**

AN AUTHENTIC ACCOUNT

OF THE

DEBATES

IN THE

HOUSE OF LORDS,

ON

TUESDAY, DECEMBER 9,

MONDAY, DECEMBER 15,

AND

WEDNESDAY, DECEMBER 17, 1783.

ON THE

BILL

"For establishing certain Regulations for the better
Management of the Territories, Revenues, and
Commerce of this Kingdom in the East-Indies."

To which is added,

AN ACCURATE LIST OF THE DIVISIONS

Both on MONDAY and WEDNESDAY.

LONDON:

Printed for J. DEBRETT, (Successor to Mr. ALMON,)
opposite BURLINGTON-HOUSE, PICCADILLY.

M.DCC.LXXXIII.

PREFACE.

THE newspapers have been so exceedingly deficient in their account of the very important debate which took place in the House of Lords on Tuesday the 9th instant, that a Gentleman who was present, and is very anxious that the Public should have as accurate an account as possible of that day's proceedings, has sent the following account to the press, in which, however, he is conscious that he has not done justice to any one of the noble speakers.

THE
DEBATE
IN THE
HOUSE of LORDS, &c.

AT half past three o'clock on Tuesday the 9th of December, Mr. Secretary Fox brought up the India Bill from the House of Commons; which being read a first time, the Duke of Portland moved that Monday next be fixed for the second reading of the bill.

Lord Thurlow immediately rose and observed that it was indeed very extraordinary that even the common forms of Parliament were

were neglected, though the bill then before their Lordships was of such infinite magnitude. By the order of their Lordships' proceedings, the House should be moved for leave to print the bill; and after that, surely the second reading of a bill of so much importance should be fixed for a distant day.

Earl Temple concurred in opinion with the noble and learned Lord.—The noble Duke his Lordship observed, had moved for several papers to be laid upon the table: He wished to ask the noble Duke if these were all the papers which his brain thought necessary to be produced.——His Lordship added, that as the subject was of the first importance, affecting the chartered rights of British subjects—affecting, nay tending totally to subvert the constitution of this country—He hoped their Lordships would not proceed but upon the most mature deliberation: he therefore trusted to the well-kown candour of the noble Duke, that he would not oppose any farther motion he might

might make for the production of such papers as to his mind seemed necessary to the elucidation of so important a subject. His Lordship declared, that he had meant on that day to move for a great number of records and papers from the India House; but not having the list in his pocket, he trusted to the honour and the candour of the noble Duke that such a motion would not be opposed on a future day.

The Duke of Portland said, he was not prepared to give a positive answer to his Lordship's question. To his mind the papers already on their Lordships' table were very sufficient to evince the absolute necessity for adopting the present measure; at the same time, he should not be against the production of farther evidence, if it should appear to the House to be necessary.

Lord Thurlow observed, that there was a very great degree of indecency in the mode of proceeding; that the subject was perhaps the moſt important that had ever been agitated in Parliament, in whatever light it was taken. In the firſt inſtance it was a moſt atrocious violation of private property—an enquiry which cut every Engliſhman to the bone; and which could only be juſtified by the ſtrongeſt neceſſity. The neceſſity, added his Lordſhip, muſt be fully and fairly proved by evidence brought to the Bar of the Houſe, and not by reports from a committee, to which he would pay as much attention as he would to the adventures of Robinſon Cruſoe. In the next place, ſuppoſing the neceſſity of an interference to be proved beyond the power of cavil, ſtill, his Lordſhip contended, that the preſent bill neither went to the correction of any exiſting evil, to the prevention of evil in future, nor to the relief of the Company's wants. It was, in fact, a moſt direct and daring attack upon the conſtitution of this country, and was a ſubverſion of the firſt principles of the Britiſh government. When, therefore, ſuch a bill was brought forward, it behoved their Lordſhips to be very accurate-

ly

ly informed of the real ſtate of the Company's affairs.

Lord Loughborough replied to Lord Thurlow. His Lordſhip ſtated, that the Charter of the Eaſt-India Company had been violated upon former occaſions. He particularly inſtanced the Regulating Act of 1773, which he diſapproved becauſe it did not go far enough. In fact, it was impoſſible to regulate the Company's affairs without an infringement of their Charter. Surely their Lordſhips muſt all agree in the propriety of ſomething being done. Look to the ſtate of the Company in England. It owes above a million ſterling to Government; bills have been drawn from India to a great amount. Let us caſt our eyes to the Company's ſettlements abroad. What ſcenes of deſolation and diſtreſs do we behold!—A prince has been driven from his palace—his treaſures have been ſeized, and he is now a fugitive through the plains of Indoſtan. Fertile provinces have been laid waſte; wars have been unneceſſarily waged;

waged; and though we have concluded a peace with the Marattas, yet this, in fact, leads us to a new war. The treaty between the English and Marattas having for its objects the conquest and partition of Tippoo Saib's dominions, may involve us in endless disputes. In short, continued his Lordship, wherever I turn my attention, I find very sufficient reasons for giving my support to the present bill, from the confused and distressed state of the East-India Company's affairs.

Lord Thurlow observed, that the noble and learned Lord had not yet given any solution to his difficulties. I ask the noble and learned Lord if he can reconcile the principle of the present bill to the principles of the British constitution, admitting even what we have as yet not the smallest cause to admit, that the necessity of an immediate interference by Parliament is apparent. The noble and learned Lord fills so high an office in two of his Majesty's courts, that I should naturally expect to see him the champion of our glorious constitution. It is not

not fitting that so great a character should meddle in the dirty pool of politics. The present bill means evidently to create a power which is unknown to the constitution. An *imperium in imperio*;—but as I abhor tyranny in all its shapes, I shall oppose most strenuously this strange attempt to destroy the true balance of our constitution. The present bill does not tend to increase the influence of the Crown; but it tends to set up a power in the kingdom which may be used in opposition to the Crown, and to the destruction of the liberties of the people. I wish to see the Crown great and respectable; but if the present bill should pass, it will be no longer worthy of a man of honour to wear. The King will, in fact, take the diadem from his own head, and place it on the head of Mr. Fox. Your Lordships have heard much of the Ninth Report of the Select Committee. That extraordinary performance has been in every body's hands.— The ingenious author states, that " The " East-India Company is in possession of a
" vast

"vast empire, with such a boundless pa-
"tronage, civil, military, marine, com-
"mercial, and financial, in every depart-
"ment of which such fortunes have been
"made as could be made no where else."—
This, my Lords, is the true description of that vast and boundless patronage, which this bill means to throw into the hands of the Minister of the present day: I speak the language of the late Marquis of Rockingham, for whom I had the highest respect and regard, and to whom I have been much obliged, when I say, that every Minister of this country will naturally strengthen his party by increasing his friends, and disposing of every office of honour or of emolument amongst those who will support his measures; with this explanation of the system on which the present Ministers act, and indeed in which all Ministers must act, let me conjure your Lordships to weigh well the consequences which will result to the constitution of this country, should the present bill pass into a law. By the fundamental principles of this constitution, the

executive

executive power of the State is placed in the hands of the Crown. We have heard much, my Lords, of late years, of the alarming increase of the influence of the Crown, I will candidly confess to your Lordships, that I have never seen the influence of the Crown too great. I wish to see the Crown great and respectable; and if the boundless patronage of the East must be taken from the Company, if regulations wisely adopted, and steadily enforced, will not be sufficient to remedy existing evils, let the boundless patronage of the East be placed where only, with safety to the constitution of this country it can be placed; in the hands of the executive government. In the last year we passed an act to prevent contractors from sitting in Parliament; but by the present bill, Mr. Fox's contractors do not even vacate their seats.—Such is the distinction between the Crown and a subject.

In the last year we passed an act to prevent Custom-house officers from voting for members of Parliament, so cautious were we to preserve the purity of the House of Commons, and to diminish the influence of the Crown; but in defiance of every principle which was then professed, no jealousy is expressed of the man who is to have in his possession the boundless patronage of the East. The doctrine advanced by the noble and learned Lord, is indeed extraordinary. He tells you that the act of 1773, was an infringement of the charter of the East India Company, but that his objection was, that it did not go far enough; and therefore he would totally destroy the charter.—The noble and learned Lord will recollect the doctrine of the King's Attorney-General, Sir Robert Sawyer, in the unconstitutional and infamous reign of Charles the IId. as detailed to us in that ministerial Gazette, that receptacle of all true intelligence; Mr. Woodfall's paper. Yet, my Lords, how was the doctrine of Sir Robert Sawyer reprobated by the Attorney-General of that day? The charter of the city of London was taken away, not because according

cording to Sir Robert Sawyer's opinion, it was for their good, but because the court was induced to declare it had been forfeited. At the Revolution, however, it was restored, and the strongest marks of abhorrence were expressed at so atrocious a deed, perpetrated under the semblance of justice. But before the House can consider this very important bill on that ground, to which every Englishman must naturally object to it, that it is directly subversive of our venerable constitution; and on that ground I challenge the noble and learned Lord to meet my argument fully and fairly, it will be necessary to consider the real state of the East India Company. Let us not be misled by reports from Committees of another House, to which, I again repeat, I pay as much attention as I would do to the history of Robinson Crusoe. Let the conduct of the East India Company be fairly and fully enquired into; let it be acquitted or condemned by evidence brought to the Bar of the House. Without entering very deep into the subject, let me reply, in a few words, to an observation which fell from a noble and learned Lord, that the Company's finances are diſtreſſed, and that they owe, at this moment, a million ſterling to the nation. When ſuch a charge is brought, will Parliament, in its juſtice, forget that the Company is reſtricted from employing that credit, which its great and flouriſhing ſituation gives to it? Will Parliament, in its juſtice, forget that all the bill-holders of the Company are willing to extend the period of payment? Will Parliament, in its juſtice, forget that ſo high is the credit of this Company, that if the reſtrictions were taken off to-morrow morning, every demand due to the State would be diſcharged? Will Parliament, in its juſtice, forget that not all the wiſdom of his Majeſty's councils, nor the united wiſdom of this country, has prevented us from being involved in a long, a dangerous, and an expenſive war? Will Parliament, in its juſtice, forget, that though we have met with loſs, misfortune, and diſgrace, in every other quarter of the globe, this delinquent Eaſt India Company has ſurmounted

the

the moſt aſtoniſhing difficulties in India? Will the juſtice of Parliament forget, that when peace was at laſt reſtored to this unfortunate country, the conqueſts of this delinquent Company were given up to prevent farther ſacrifices in the Weſt? Will Parliament, in its juſtice, forget that this delinquent Company, by the additional expence of freight, or captures at ſea, has ſuſtained a loſs of two millions, ſeven hundred thouſand pounds, in conſequence of our national war? Will Parliament, in its juſtice, forget, that when this country has encreaſed its debt above one hundred millions ſterling, this delinquent Company wants but a little time to pay all it owes to the Exchequer, or privilege to uſe its flowing credit? Will Parliament, in its juſtice forget that at a former period, when its commerce was circumſcribed, when it had not an empire to ſupport, this delinquent Company was allowed to iſſue bonds to the amount of three millions ſterling, though now limited, at the cloſe of an extenſive and calamitous war, to the ſum of fifteen hundred thouſand pounds?

pounds? These are circumstances which must be recollected, when we mean to violate private property—an injury which must cut every Englishman to the bone, and which nothing but the strongest necessity, fully and fairly proved, can ever justify. The noble and learned Lord has mentioned the depopulation of fertile provinces in India, the expulsion of a king from his palace, and the cruelties exercised upon an old woman. These, my Lords, are founding words, but I call upon the noble and learned Lord to prove the facts.—It is something singular, that when the character of Mr. Hastings is thus held up to public detestation, his name should be cautiously suppressed. Whence, my Lords, this remarkable degree of delicacy towards Mr. Hastings? If he is a desolator of provinces; if he is a plunderer, and an enemy to the human race, let him be punished for his crimes, but let the facts be proved. The little, low, dirty attempts of malice and faction, which have long been employed to destroy the character of that great man (as

I

I think him) can have no weight with your Lordships. How industriously, my Lords, has every transaction of Mr. Hastings's long government, that could tend to criminate him, been circulated? The reports of a Committee have been sold as pamphlets. The ingenuity of some men, the industry and the warm imagination of others, have been long employed to sully the well earned reputation of Mr. Hastings. To my mind, my Lords, Mr. Hastings is one of the most extraordinary characters that this country has ever produced. He has served the East-India Company thirty three years in the most important situations, twelve years as Governor, or Governor-General of Bengal. He is a man, my Lords, whose integrity, whose honour, whose firmness of mind, and whose perseverance, are not only very generally acknowledged in this kingdom, and in Asia, but throughout the continent of Europe. He is a man, my Lords, who possesses a most extensive knowledge of the languages, the politics, the customs, and the revenues

of

of Hindoſtan. He is a man, my Lords, who infuſed the ſpirit which animated his own mind, and roſe ſuperior to the aſtoniſhing difficulties he had to encounter into the breaſts of our brave and intrepid countrymen, who have ſo nobly diſtinguiſhed themſelves in Aſia. Mr. Haſtings is a man, my Lords, who has re-eſtabliſhed peace in India, who furniſhed reſources for the war while it laſted, by an increaſe of revenue in Bengal, and has preſerved the provinces under his more immediate control in peace and tranquillity. Mr. Haſtings is a man, my Lords, who has held a bold and conſiſtent language throughout. When the Government of this country ſent three men to thwart and to oppoſe all his meaſures, he deſired either to be recalled or confirmed. Would to God thoſe men had never arrived there. When I conſider the ſcene of confuſion that enſued, the factious, perſonal, and party ſpirit, by which they were actuated from the very hour of their landing, I am aſtoniſhed that Mr. Haſtings has been able to ſurmount ſo arduous a trial.

What

What have been the means, my Lords, to which Mr. Hastings has had recourse to preserve his power? Has he employed the low and dirty arts of intrigue, which have heretofore been practised?

No, my Lords, he has been supported by the voice of the public — by great and meritorious actions! This being my opinion of Mr. Hastings, I shall support him until evidence of his delinquency shall be produced. Whence, my Lords, this extreme desire to avoid a full and pure discussion of this question? I again repeat it; if Mr. Hastings is guilty, recall him, punish him; but do not, my Lords, let us be deluded by tales fabricated for the purpose of the hour, and circulated with a degree of industry which disgraces the honour and dignity of the British nation. I cannot help adding, my Lords, that to my mind the late dispatches from India contain such convincing proofs of the vigour of our Government in Bengal, of the regulations formed for the collection of the revenues,

and

and the administration of justice throughout the provinces, added to the œconomical arrangements formed in the civil and military departments, that I do believe it will not be in the power of any clerk in office, that Mr. Fox's Directors may send out, to throw Bengal into confusion again in less than two or three years.

Lord Townshend then observed, that the question then before their Lordships was undoubtedly of the utmost importance. The measure was bold and rapid; for his part, his Lordship said, he loved bold and rapid measures, when the necessity for such measure was evident. He conjured their Lordships to consider the state of the East-India Company's affairs both at home and abroad, and that they would resist every attempt to create an unnecessary delay.

Lord Temple observed, that he did not mean to protract or to delay the consideration

tion of the present bill: he trusted, indeed, that a bill so dangerous in its principle, so subversive of the constitution, could never pass that House. The papers his Lordship meant to move for, were absolutely necessary, provided the bill was to come under their Lordships' consideration.

Lord Townshend rose to disavow any reflection upon the last noble speaker, in what he had said.

The Earl of Derby expressed his perfect acquiescence in the opinion of the noble Lord (Thurlow:) his Lordship said, it would be impossible to determine upon the justice and injustice of the present measure, without going very fully into the conduct of the Company, and its chief servant, Mr. Hastings. This, his Lordship pledged himself to the House, he would do on a future day.

Lord Loughborough then rose and observed, that as there was, in fact, no question

tion before the House, he must apologize to their Lordships for taking up a few minutes of their time, in reply to what fell from the noble and learned Lord. With respect to what the learned Lord had said of Mr. Hastings, he begged to observe, that he meant neither to dispute nor to cement the very warm eulogium he had passed upon that gentleman. Indeed he thought the merits or demerits of Mr. Hastings, made no part of the present business: it was a defective system that he wished to correct; and Mr. Hastings himself had complained that the present system was defective. His Lordship declared, that he wished, therefore, to put Mr. Hastings entirely out of the question in the discussion of the present business. He trusted the learned Lord would thank him for giving him an opportunity of explaining a very harsh expression which he had used. The late Sir John Clavering and Colonel Monson were men of as strict integrity, and as high a sense of their honour, as this country had ever produced. They had sacrificed

ficed their lives in the public service; and, surely, when their names were mentioned, it should only be with that degree of respect which is due to their great and exalted characters. With respect to the gentleman (Mr. Francis) who had returned to this country, he believed his abilities were universally allowed; nor had his Lordship ever heard the smallest reflection cast upon his integrity, or honourable conduct, from the time he went abroad until he returned. These three gentlemen were sent to Bengal; Mr. Hastings and Mr. Barwell, who then stood high in the opinion of his Majesty's Ministers, were associated with them in the government, because it was necessary that some of the old servants of the Company should have a share in the administration of their affairs. Disputes unfortunately broke out; and from a variety of causes, needless now to relate, though both parties certainly called for a decisive determination on the subject of those disputes, none were ever sent. This, however, his Lordship observed, is foreign to the subject before the
House.

House. With respect to the production of farther papers, the necessity did not then strike him. His Lordship said, that the business of India, for the last ten years, was as well known as the campaigns of the Duke of Marlborough. Every bookseller's shop was full of India tracts; and the House was certainly as competent to judge now, as they could be ten months hence, of the propriety or impropriety of the present bill. With respect to the doctrine adopted by Sir Robert Sawyer, in the reign of Charles the Second, he could assure the learned Lord, that he entertained as strong sentiments of abhorrence for such a doctrine, as the noble and learned Lord could do.

Lord Thurlow. I am much obliged to the noble and learned Lord for the opportunity he has given me for retracting an hasty and intemperate expression. I do not, however, feel myself at all inclined to retract it: your Lordships know perfectly well, that I was not speaking of the gentle-

gentlemen who are deceafed as private characters. In that view I go along with the noble and learned Lord moft fincerely; but fpeaking of them as public men, I fay their arrival in India was a public misfortune, and would to God they had not arrived there! If I wanted a convincing proof of the juftice of my former fentiments, the noble and learned Lord has given me one. He tells your Lordfhips that thefe gentlemen were fent to India; and that Mr. Haftings and Mr. Barwell were affociated with them, becaufe it was neceffary to employ fome perfons of experience in the Company's affairs. Thefe three gentlemen, by the learned Lord's confeffion, went out as a party from this country; and as a party they acted, from the very day, from the very hour of their landing in Bengal. It is the confequences which refulted from a fyftematic oppofition to the government of Mr. Haftings that I deplore. It was that fyftematic oppofition which has prevented this country from benefiting, as it would otherwife have done, by the

great

great and splendid talents of Mr. Hastings; and I am astonished how the superior mind even of that great man, has been able to bear up against the attempts of malice, party, and faction, so industriously excited to disgrace him for the last eight years of his life. The noble and learned Lord declares, that the merits and demerits of Mr. Hastings are not to be included in the discussion of the present bill. Good God, my Lords, what language is this? The learned Lord described the consequences of various acts, of which Mr. Hastings is said to be the author; and shall we shrink from, or blink the fair question? Let Mr. Hastings rise or fall by his merits: it is impossible to avoid a full discussion of his conduct, and of the Company's management. Has it yet been proved, my Lords, that disorders of an alarming magnitude prevail in India? The East-India Company declare, that by the exertions of their servants abroad, and their Directors at home, they have repelled the efforts of all their enemies to subdue them; and that the calamities,

mities which have happened, unfortunate and diſtreſſing as they are undoubtedly, are inſeparable from a ſtate of war. Shall we, my Lords, be borne down by the tide of faction, party, or ſelf-intereſt? Let us firſt prove the extent of the evil, and then it will be time enough to conſider the nature of the mode propoſed for the prevention of ſuch an evil in future. I will not do ſo great an injuſtice to the character of the noble Duke, as to ſuppoſe, for a moment, that his Grace is capable of adopting that line of conduct now, which he ſo ſeverely reprobated in Miniſters on a former occaſion. The noble Duke will, doubtleſs, be deſirous of tranſmitting his name with honour to poſterity; and whatever may be the opinion of other noble Lords, his Grace, I am ſure, will co-operate cordially in giving the preſent ſubject a full, a liberal, and a free diſcuſſion.

The Duke of Richmond, in very ſevere and pointed terms, condemned the preſent bill. His Grace contended that it was the unhappy interference of Ministers which had produced the present mischiefs. The Company, when left to itself, was great and flourishing; and the advice he formerly gave regarding the cursed American war, he would give upon the present measure — Begin by undoing all you have done, and leave the Company to themselves. His Grace then lamented the fatal Coalition which had taken place some months ago — To that he attributed the present unconstitutional measure — That baneful Coalition, he said, had induced many very worthy men to believe that there was not a grain of public virtue in the nation; and surely the present measure would tend most strongly to confirm that opinion. His Grace then adverted to the line which the Duke of Portland had taken in 1773, when a measure of a very inferior degree of atrocity indeed was proposed by the Ministers of that day. How was it possible he could support such a measure without a sacrifice of every principle he had formerly professed? One of these three consequences must result,

as

as his Grace obferved, from the unnatural Coalition — The Duke of Portland muft give up his principles to Lord North, or Lord North muft yield his to the Duke of Portland, or both muft facrifice their principles to their intereft. His Grace profeffed his high opinion of the honour of the Duke of Portland; but he had been mifled and deceived by his hireling dependants, otherwife it was impoffible he could now fupport a fyftem which he had formerly condemned in fuch ftrong terms.

The Duke of Portland rofe, and, with warmth and energy, denied that he had changed his principles; he ftill adhered to them, and fubfcribed moft heartily to the fentiments of the protefts which he had figned in 1773. Circumftances however had changed — and the prefent bill was neceffary, in order to fave the Eaft-India Company and the nation from ruin — Such was the fituation of the Company, that fomething muft be done. He defired the noble Duke, before he made fuch reflec-

tions

tions on his conduct, to confider ferioufly the ftate of the country at the time the Coalition took place—What would have been the confequence if that event had not been brought about, no man would venture to fay.

The Duke of Richmond again rofe, to reply to the obfervations of the noble Duke. He totally denied the exiftence of fuch a neceffity now, or, indeed, that fuch a neceffity fhould ever exift, as would compel the Legiflature of this country to deftroy the rights of their fellow fubjects without even an enquiry. He lamented that his Grace had fo entirely changed his principles. The Duke then read from a paper, the feveral motions which had been made for papers by his Grace in the year 1773; and he proved that his Grace now held that language which he had formerly condemned.—A perufal of the proteft which the Duke of Portland had formerly figned, was a pledge to pofterity of his principles. If he now altered his opinion, pofterity would

judge

judge of the motives for such a conduct. The Duke of Richmond said he gloried in having signed that protest: he said he should act with consistency on this, and, he hoped, on every other occasion. The baneful system which he had reprobated in 1773, he should firmly oppose in 1783. For his part, he neither wished the Crown nor the Minister to possess the boundless patronage of the East: but of this he was sure, that the present bill militated against every principle of the Constitution. The arguments adduced, both within doors and without, to justify the measure, were indeed most curious; because Lord North very unjustifiably enjoyed a small part of the patronage of the East in secret, we will therefore give the Minister the whole in the face of day. His Grace then went fully into Lord North's management of the East-India Company, through his secretary, Mr. Robinson: he said, Lord North had nominated Directors in many instances, and all the evil that had happened was owing to his interference — That unhappy man, continued

tinued his Grace, was surely born to be the ruin of this country — To him we owe the American war — To him we owe the misfortunes of the East-India Company — That Company was great and flourishing in 1773, when its constitution was broke in upon — From that time the Minister is responsible for all that has happened. Admitting, with the learned Lord, (Loughborough) that Mr. Hastings has been culpable, how often and how earnestly has he called upon Lord North to remove him, if he disapproved of his conduct? Admitting, on the other hand, that Mr. Hastings, under every obstruction, has saved India, and that there is a fair prospect of peace and tranquillity in our possessions. — Lord North is responsible for not having decided between the contending parties; so that in whatever light the subject is viewed, it is to a want of vigour and resolution in the late Minister, and to a desire of acquiring patronage without responsibility, that the misfortunes in India have been owing. The only remedy, his Grace added, which

promises

promises to be successful, is, to free the Company from the vexatious interference of Ministers — To prevent their relations or their dependants from getting to India, and they will soon extricate themselves from all their difficulties.

The Earl of Carlisle earnestly pressed their Lordships to proceed on the important business of India, with as much speed as possible. He described the distress of the Company at home, and the confusion that reigned abroad, nearly in the same terms with Lord Loughborough; and he expressed his firm conviction, that nothing but the interposition of Parliament could prevent this country from being deeply involved in the ruin of the East-India Company.

Lord Sydney professed his entire disapprobation of the principle of the bill. It went, his Lordship said, to the erection of an influence more dangerous than the influence of the Crown, and was directly

rectly subversive of the constitution. His Lordship then adverted to a very extraordinary language that had been uttered, that this bill had passed the Lower House by a very great majority, and therefore it came with additional strength to their Lordships. He had spent the greatest part of his life in the Lower House, and no man held that House in greater respect than he did; but he begged their Lordships to recollect, that measures which, in their consequences, had ruined this nation, were carried by a still greater majority than the present. He alluded to the progressive steps taken in support of the cursed American war for two years and upwards. After dwelling upon this for some time, with great force of argument, his Lordship intreated the House not to be led away by majorities in another House, but to determine on the only ground on which a measure could surely be determined upon, its merits or demerits.

Lord

Lord Abingdon spoke next, in a stile of great warmth: he said the bill deserved every injurious epithet he could bestow upon it; that it was not only founded in injustice, and a public robbery, but a treasonable bill, and whoever supported such a bill, was guilty of treason to the constitution. His Lordship was proceeding, when Lord Townshend called him to order. Lord Abingdon contented himself with declaring he was not disorderly; and that if he was again called to order, he would move to read the protest signed by the Duke of Portland in 1773.

Earl Temple then moved for leave to present a petition from the East India Company. The petition was brought up and read; and the House adjourned about half an hour after eight o'clock.

MONDAY, *December* 15.

About three o'clock the Earl of Abingdon rose, and observed that if the attendance of their Lordships had been then more numerous, he should have submitted to their consideration some remarks and subsequent propositions relative to the East-India bill, and other points of great importance; but he must beg leave to defer these until the house should become more filled.

Many Peers entering soon afterwards, the Earl of Abingdon rose again, and said,

My Lords, the moment being now arrived when we are called upon, not only by the voice of the nation, but by the peculiar characteristic of this House, the feelings of our own honour, to exercise that function which the Constitution of the country hath placed in us; I mean, my Lords, that of holding between the King and people the balance of the State in the scale of its government; or, as Charles the First used to express it, "of being that excellent screen between the Prince and the people, to assist each against the encroachments of the other."

It

It is, therefore, that I rise, and before any other proceedings are had upon the bill that is now before us, for " vesting the affairs of the East-India Company in the hands of certain Directors," to trouble your Lordships with a very few words, as introductory to a motion which I mean to have the honour of submitting to your Lordships' consideration.

My Lords, the bill before us, " for " vesting the affairs of the East-India Com- " pany in the hands of certain Directors," is, in a threefold manner, now under the contemplation of this House; and it is so, my Lords, first, in address and appeal to us in our legislative capacities, in common with the two other branches of the legislature.

Secondly, in address and appeal to us as the Supreme Court of Judicature, or dernier resort of justice, distinct from the two other branches of the legislature, and appertaining to ourselves.

F 2

And,

And, thirdly, my Lords, in that capacity, in that peculiar and diftinguifhed capacity to which I have juft alluded, the capacity of being the mediator between the King and the people, and of rendering juftice to both, by oppofing as well the encroachments of the Crown upon the liberties of the fubject, as the encroachments of the fubject upon the juft prerogative of the Crown.

Of the two former, my Lords, our legiflative and judiciary capacities, and our duties therein upon this occafion, I fhall not now take up any of your Lordfhips' time, nor, I truft, fhall I have any future occafion to do fo; but it is to the third, our mediation between the Crown and its fubjects, grounded upon the prefent neceffity of our interference, that at this moment leads me to call for your Lordfhips' attention.

Of the bill, my Lords, of which I have fpoken, your Lordfhips having read it, it

is

is unneceſſary for me to enter into the detail of its particulars; indeed it is not the time for me to do ſo, and I muſt again hope, that that time will never arrive. But it is to its principle that I am now to look; and, in ſo doing, enough and enough remains to occupy the deepeſt and moſt ſolemn reflections of this Houſe; for, in this view of the bill, what is it that your Lordſhips have to ſee, but a bill that has for its ſubject-matter, propoſitions as fatal to the juſt prerogative of the Crown, by their adoption, as by their effects they will be found ruinous to, and ſubverſive of the rights, liberties, and properties of the ſubject. Propoſitions, as unique in themſelves, as they are unmatched in the annals of our hiſtory. Propoſitions, big with ambition, with ambition no leſs violent than that which filled the mind of Cromwell, and brought the head of Charles the Firſt to the block. No leſs violent did I ſay, my Lords? Ten times more violent, more daring, more enterpriſing! For, in the caſe of *that* Cromwell, he had ſome

ground

ground to stand upon, he had arguments to offer, he had reasons to assign, he had, at least, that plea of tyrants, the plea of necessity for what he did; for, in the words of Lord Bolingbroke, he had this to say, either that "Charles the First must lose his head, or England lose its liberties."

But in the case of the Cromwell of this bill, what has he to urge for that which he has done? What ground has he to stand upon, what arguments to offer, what reasons to assign, what plea of necessity to state? A plea of necessity, it is true, he had: he stated to the House of Commons, that the East-India Company was bankrupt; it was false in statement, it was false in proof. But I admit the truth of both; and yet, whence arose the necessity of subverting the constitution of this country, by placing the executive power of Government in the hands of a mountebank Secretary of State? A Secretary of State who does not shrink back from declaring, that he is not the King's Minister, but the Minister of the

People;

People; who glories in the diſtinction, who fortifies himſelf under it in the Houſe in which he acts. And yet, my Lords, no more the Miniſter of the People, than I the friend of his politics! The Miniſter, it is true, of a corrupt majority of the Houſe of Commons, where the people now are, as he ſays; but not the Miniſter of the People, as when mounted on his ſtage at Covent-Garden, and in Weſtminſter-Hall.

But, I ſay, my Lords, whence aroſe the neceſſity of this ſubverſion of the Conſtitution? Whence aroſe the neceſſity of erecting a new power in the State—a middle power between the King and people, on the one hand holding the King in chains, and on the other ruling the people, through the medium of a corrupt majority in Parliament, with a rod of iron? And yet, my Lords, this is the propoſition *in totidem verbis*: a propoſition to wreſt the reins of Government out of the hands of the executive power, and to place it in the hands of
a ſelf-

a self-created demagogue, supported by a factious and desperate cabal; a proposition therefore no less injurious to the people, than at the same time furnishing the most direct attack upon Majesty that the annals of our history afford; a proposition, as I have said, more daring even than that which brought the head of Charles the First to the block, because less founded: a proposition of ambition no less glaring, but, I trust, my Lords, less hopeful, for it is ours to prevent it.

But, my Lords, it has been said of this bill, on the one side, that it will increase the influence of the Crown; and it has been cunningly and craftily not denied on the other. But this is not the truth, my Lords; I deny the fact; the reverse is the truth. This bill is not to increase the influence of the Crown; it is to destroy it. It is, I admit, to obtain an influence; but an influence as poisonous to the just influence and legal prerogative of the Crown, as it is deadly to the rights and liberties of the people.

And

And when I say this, my Lords, let it not be thought that I speak rashly and unadvisedly upon the subject, that I talk without book, that I reason without my host, that I am unsupported in what I say; I speak, my Lords, to the sense and knowledge of the House; for, my Lords, that to pull down the influence of the Crown has been the long unremitting endeavours of the Minister of the people and his Whig connections, as they are called, (for of his Tory coalition I shall presently speak) the House wants no information. The facts of this speak for themselves. We have seen bills of Reform upon bills of Reform to this end passing into acts of the Legislature; bills taking away from the splendour of the Crown, no less necessary to Majesty than the birthright of the Prince; bills meanly and ignominiously descending into the very kitchen and cellar of the King, there to retrench and deprive his Majesty of the very comforts and provisions of his table. Can it then, my Lords, even in supposition, be thought, that those who have done this,

can

can now have any view or intention to throw the wealth of the East into the lap of the Throne? No, my Lords; the very suppofition is abfurdity itfelf: befides, the bill ftates the contrary. For four years certain, the Crown has nothing to do with it; and give me a leafe for four years of fuch means of corruption as thefe are, and I muft be, what the Minifter of the people is not, a very filly fellow indeed, if I don't purchafe a fee fimple in the premifes for ever after.

But this is not all, my Lords; for let us look for demonftration upon this fubject to the tenets and principles of this party of men. And in doing this, let us look to their creed, in a well-known publication of theirs, called "Thoughts on the prefent Difcontents;" and then look to their practice upon that creed. Look to their creed, and there you will find, that whilft it pulls the influence of the Crown down to the ground, it fets up another influence ten times more dangerous—ten times more de-

ftructive

structive to the constitution. The influence of an Aristocracy, or to express it in their own words, the influence of connection; and of which this creed speaking, says, " In one of the most fortunate peri-
" ods of our history, this country was go-
" verned by a connection; I mean the
" great connection of Whigs in the reign
" of Queen Anne." Such is this influence, my Lords. The influence of an Oligarchical junto in the two Houses of Parliament, holding, as I have said, the King captive in the one hand, and with the other ruling the people, not by the fundamental laws of the land, but after the manner of this bill, by laws " of mere political dif-
" cretion only," and subversive of their rights, liberties, and properties.

But, my Lords, let us now look to their practice upon this creed; and here, I am aware, I am anticipated by the House, and that the day which stains, and will continue everlastingly to stain the journals of Parliament, I mean the 17th day of Feb-

February last, is uppermost in the thoughts, and present to the minds of every one of your Lordships. A day of connection, my Lords, a day, when by an infamous and wicked connection of principles, not the connection of *idem sentire de republicâ*, which alone is or can be the basis of all well intentioned political union, but of the most jarring factions, a connection which one might have thought no chemistry either on earth or in heaven could ever have brought together: I say, my Lords, a day when his Majesty was besieged in his Cabinet; when he was told the appointment of his own domestic servants did not lie in him; when his Majesty resisted; but when after a six-weeks resistance, with a fortitude of mind that will add lustre to his reign, he fell a victim to this connection.

And thus, my Lords, has the theory of these politics been now reduced to practice; for such have been the effects of this connection, which is now sought by this bill. Not the influence of the King's Minister

for

for the King, but of the King's Minister against the King. Of the King's Minister, who, if this bill passes, may say to the King, I am the Minister of this country, and let my conduct be what it will, let my insults to you be what they may, it is not in your power, it is what you dare not do, it is not for you to remove me.

But, my Lords, that I may trespass no longer on the time and patience of the House, the motion which I shall have the honour to submit to your Lordships is this:—

That the Judges may be summoned to attend this House, in order to give their advice in point of law, upon the bill now depending in Parliament " for vesting the affairs of the East-India Company in the hands of certain Directors," &c.

And here, my Lords, whilst, as the ground of this motion, I take the liberty of stating to your Lordships the queries,

queries, which (as neceſſary to my information at leaſt) I ſhall propound to the Judges for their counſel and advice; ſo by this motion, will an opportunity be afforded to the Houſe, of having any other difficulties reſolved in point of law, which may occur to any other individuals of your Lordſhips.

My Lords, the query is this:

Whether by the commiſſion, as ſet up in the bill for veſting the affairs of the Eaſt-India Company in the hands of certain directors, an executive power be not thereby inſtituted, new in the government, and unknown to the conſtitution of the country; and whether that executive power be not as well derogatory to the Crown, and hurtful to the juſt, legal, and royal prerogative of the King, as dangerous to the rights, liberties, and properties of the ſubject?

Now, my Lords, in putting this query to the Judges, I find myſelf no leſs upheld therein by the ſpirit of the conſtitution,
than

than confirmed by the letter of the law; by the fpirit of the conftitution, my Lords, as handed down to us by the very ingenious and learned author of the fpirit of laws; who, fpeaking of the Englifh conftitution, fays that the executive power ought to be in the hands of a monarch: becaufe this branch of government, which has always need of expedition, is better adminiftered by one than by many: whereas whatever depends on the legiflative power is oftentimes better regulated by many than by a fingle perfon. Again: But if there was no monarch, fays he, and the executive power was committed to a certain number of perfons felected from the legiflative body, there would be an end of liberty; by reafon the two powers would be united, as the fame perfons would actually fometimes have, and would moreover be always able to have, a fhare in both. And as confirmed by the letter of the law, in as much as, by the ftatute of the 16th of Charles I. ch. 1, a power being lodged in the Chancellor (in cafe of the King's default)

fault) to call Parliaments; and if he failed, then in the Peers, or any twelve of them, and if they failed, then in the Sheriffs; it was said by the Judges of those days, that this was a direct breach of the original constitution; for it introduced into the monarchy a kind of republic, by setting up a supreme power, besides the regal power, and inconsistent with it. Of the statute too of the 15th of Charles I. chap. 5, whereby it was enacted, that that Parliament then sitting should not be dissolved, prorogued, or adjourned but by Act of Parliament, it was said, that this was another breach of that constitution, which had originally established the King's prerogative in that particular; and therefore these two acts were, early in the next reign, repealed.

The second query is,

Whether the immediate creative act of any charter of incorporation is not vested in the King by virtue of his royal prerogative? And if yes: Whether by the forfeiture

ture or diffolution of fuch charter, its franchifes are not revertible to the Crown, in order to be re-granted by the King if neceffary? And if fo, Whether the commiffion of Directors appointed by this bill be not an encroachment upon the royal prerogative of the Crown?

Sir William Blackftone fpeaking of the erecting of corporations by the King, as the fountain of privilege, fays, "I now only mention them incidently, in order to remark the King's prerogative in making them; which is grounded upon this foundation, that the King having the fole adminiftration of the government in his hands, is the beft and the only judge, in what capacities, with what privileges, and under what diftinctions his people are the beft qualified to ferve, and to act under him."

The third query is,

Whether, confiftent with the judicial capacity of this Houfe, the disfranchifing of a corporation of such magnitude as that of the East-India Company, the reasons of such disfranchisement ought not to be proved and supported at the bar of the House by the strongest and most entire evidence? Or, whether consistently with the duty of this House to the King, as the hereditary Counsellors of the Crown, a bill creative of a new executive power, in violation of the royal prerogative, ought not to be rejected *in limine* upon its principle, and without entering into the merits of it.

My Lords, when Charles II. and James II. seized upon the charters, which they did for the purposes of the state, as they said, although, says Sir William Blackstone, the proceedings in most of them were sufficiently regular, it gave great and just offence: But it seems Charles James Fox can now of himself attempt what those tyrants, neither Charles nor James Stuart put together dared to do, seize upon charters by force and violence.

The fourth query is,

Whether if this bill should pass both Houses of Parliament, encroaching as it does upon the undoubted prerogative of the Crown, it be not a right inherent in the King, as well as a duty which he owes to the country in preservation of the constitution, to put his negative upon such bill?

Baron Montsequieu says, " the executive power ought to have a share in the legislature by the power of rejecting, otherwise it would be soon stripped of its prerogative. But should the legislative power usurp a share of the excutive, the latter would be equally undone." Again, " if the Prince," says he, " were to have a share in the legislature by the power of resolving, liberty would be lost. But as it is necessary he should have a share in the legislature for the support of his own prerogative, this share must consist in the power of rejecting." Sir William Blackstone, too, says, " the King is a constituent part of the supreme legislative legiflative power; and, as fuch, has the prerogative of rejecting fuch provifions in Parliament, as he judges improper to be paffed." He fays, too, fpeaking of the encroachment of the legiflative upon the executive power: " Thus the long Parliament of Charles I. while it acted in a conftitutional manner with the royal concurrence, redreffed many heavy grievances, and eftablifhed many falutary laws: But when the two Houfes affumed the power of legiflation, in exclufion of the royal authority, they foon after affumed likewife the reins of adminiftration; and in confequence of thefe united powers, overturned both church and ftate, and eftablifhed a worfe oppreffion than any they pretended to remedy.

And now, my Lords, thefe being the queries which it is my intention to fubmit to the opinion of the judges, together with my reafons for thefe queries, I fhall now beg leave to add one reafon more for the motion itfelf, of calling for the advice of the judges upon this occafion; and it is

this,

this, that, as if the opinion of the judges had been taken upon the question of the American war, before it was entered into, that is, whether the Parliament of England had a right to levy taxes internally on America, America not being represented in the Parliament of England, that country might at this time have been a part of the British empire; so upon the same ground am I persuaded that the putting of these questions to the judges now, may be the means of saving the East Indies to this country: For, my Lords, is it to be supposed, that the servants of the East-India Company in India, connected as they are in the interest with the Company here, together with Mr. Hastings, at the head of an hundred thousand men there, will quietly deliver up those possessions, when by that delivery, they know that they are themselves to be displaced, to make room for others; and if not displaced, that they will have members of Parliament, and members of Parliament's sons and kindred riding upon them four and five deep, and quartered

upon

upon their emoluments, as much without number as without reason.

And now, my Lords, I have done; asking pardon of the House for this long trespass on their patience, and, whilst sitting down, not doubting but that your Lordships will think that a monopoly of power, such as this bill requires, is not only unfit, under any circumstances whatever, to be had, but that if it were fit, to place it in the hands of him who seeks it, would be as unsafe for, as dangerous to the constitution of the country, I shall hope that the motion which I shall now have the honour to submit to the House, will meet with the concurrence of your Lordships.

In that part of the speech where the words Charles James Fox were introduced,

Lord Derby rose, and called the noble Lord to order. He said it was unusual to introduce the name of a member of the House of Commons into a debate.

When the Order of the Day was called for,

The Duke of Richmond called the attention of their Lordships to a petition, which he presented from the city of London. It was conceived, his Grace observed, under the greatest apprehensions for their franchises, and expressed in very strong language. He therefore thought it should be read. It was read accordingly.

The purport of the petition was, That a bill pending before their Lordships, threatened an extinction of their privileges, held up an awful precedent of violated charters, and, by aiming at the confiscation of public, menanced every species of private property. It therefore prayed, that such a bill might not pass into a law; that their Lordships would interfere and save them from the grasp of power, which, in this instance, appeared to them so singularly dangerous and alarming.

The Duke of Manchester felt dissatisfied with some of the expressions in this petition. They sounded harsh to his ear; they were, in his mind, violent, and not sufficiently guarded and decent for the occasion. He migh, however, have mistaken the literal phraseology. It seemed to him a very strong accusation of the other House, and he was not sure how far it became one branch of the Legislature to suffer an arraignment of another at their Bar. He wished, for these reasons, to read the petition to their Lordships, and was sorry on having done so, to find his exceptions so well founded.

The Duke of Richmond was much surprised to hear such a language from his Grace; for the very words used by the city of London on this occasion, were to be found in a protest on their Lordships Journals, signed by the names of Rockingham and Portland; and he little expected to hear their mode of expression censured from such a quarter. The petitions from America had

had been rejected on similar grounds. Besides, was it not the constitution of this country, that subjects had a right to petition against whatever they considered as a grievance? No matter, said his Grace, who your petitioners are, whether corporate or not, or against whom they complain, whether against the Minister or the House of Commons; the laws of the land give them a right to state their grievances to your Lordships; and your Lordships will not accommodate your decisions according to the fundamental principles of the constitution, if you do not give them a hearing.

The Duke of Manchester said the noble Duke certainly knew him too well to need any explanation of his principles, or to doubt of his conviction concerning the people's right to petition Parliament. Nor had he intimated any other objection than what was suggested, not by the matter but by the manner of it. The noble Duke had also mistated the argument on which the American petition was thrown out. For the Miniftry of that day infifted againft admitting the petition, only becaufe no Lord would pledge himfelf to the Houfe, that it allowed the right of taxation to the Britifh Parliament. His Grace, however, did not chufe to infift on the validity of his objection, and the petition was ordered to lie on the table.

The Order of the Day was then called for, and Mr. Rous and Mr. Dallas appeared as Counfel for the Eaft-India Company; Mr. Hardinge and Mr. Plomer as Counfel for the Directors.

Mr. Rous opened the caufe of his clients in a very mafterly manner. He ftated, in very warm and expreffive language, the enormity and the injuftice of the prefent bill. He obferved that as there was no fpecific charge brought againft his conftituents, he would be under the neceffity of proving their merits with the public by evidence at the Bar of the Houfe, and to

prove

prove the actual situation of India, by the last advices. Under the first head, Mr. Rous stated, that the additional customs paid by the East-India Company, for fifteen years, were the acquitments of the Dewannee, and exceeded the sum of the fifteen years antecedent to that period, in the sum of five millions sterling. That the sum paid by the Company to the public, as their participation of the territorial revenues, was three millions sterling; so in fact the Company was, to this moment, a considerable loser by the territorial acquisitions, though the nation had been a gainer; for the sums expended by the Company in acquiring those revenues, exceeded their receipts in the sum of five millions and upwards. But the acquisition of the Dewannee had, in every point of view, been a most important object to the British nation. Mr. Rous then stated, that the exports from this country since the territorial acquisitions, had amounted last June to about five hundred thousand pounds. He next remarked upon the flourishing state of the Company's credit, and said, that if Parliament would give them leave to borrow, their debt to the state would instantly be paid off. The credit of the Company could only be destroyed by the passing of the present bill. Mr. Rous then said he would bring evidence to prove, that in Bengal, Bahar, Benares, and Oude, we enjoyed profound peace, a firm government, an encreasing revenue, and had effected a reduction of expences. The Carnatic was evacuated. The account of the peace had arrived in India, and all hostilities had ceased between us and the French. That peace was concluded on such terms with the Marattas as must make it lasting; and such was Tippoo Saib's situation, that he had undoubtedly made peace with us, under the terms of the Sixteenth Article of the Treaty of Peace. Of this Mr. Rous said he was so confident, that he would forfeit his head if it was not the case. After dwelling very fully on these several heads, Mr. Rous proceeded to call in witnesses.

The

The evidence continued for feveral hours. The charters, acts of Parliament, grants, and other authentic documents of the Company's tenure and ftate, were read. The evidence was claffed under feparate heads, and evidence, written and oral, brought to each point. When the Counfel came to propofe, to prove that peace was reftored to the Carnatic,

Lord Loughborough rofe and faid, he was perfectly fatisfied that their Lordfhips would agree with him, that much of the evidence which had been exhibited, was at leaft irrelative and unapplicable to the nature and tendency of the bill now under the confideration of the Houfe. The whole hiftory of the Company's eftablifhment had come to their Lordfhips' knowledge under the fhape of evidence. But how would fuch a complicated narrative make againft the plan for re-eftablifhing the interefts of the Company on a new and permanent foundation? What was proved by that ftatement which their Lordfhips did not already

ready know, or about which one noble Lord in the House entertained a single doubt? Was any friend of this measure inclined to call in question the Company's right to their territorial possessions in India? To what purpose then detain their Lordships with a detail of their chartered rights, and the variety of grants obtained by them from several Indian powers? Surely there was but little information in all this; and whatever it was, the House seemed but little disposed to be benefited by it. Still the species of evidence on which Counsel were now entering, seemed least of all adapted to the business before the House. For what had the question in issue to do with the news of a peace establishment in the Carnatic? It was, in his opinion, perfectly unnatural to the bill, whether there were peace or war. It did not depend on the present, but the past. It was not so much what the Company is, as what the Company has done, that furnished a plea for such a bill, which therefore, if properly founded, could not be affected by any
situation

situation of their affairs, however promising or prosperous. He had long waited for the discretion of Counsel; but it did not appear, that they seemed inclined to come to any precise conclusion on their evidence.

From these considerations, he was satisfied the very odd arrangement of evidence which the Counsel for the Company had thus submitted to their Lordships attention, could serve no other purpose on earth than to protract the business now under discussion. And his Lordship begged leave to remind their Lordships, that the time of the bill was very precious, whether it succeeded or not. From the dispatches that might naturally be expected to have been sent, the minds of the people in the Indies would be full of suspense. Nothing would be done till the plan under contemplation of Parliament was either authenticated or rejected. An end, we might well suppose, would for the present be put to every kind of business — but he understood from rumour, nay, he had been informed so since he came into the

House,

House, that Counsel had directions to protract this bill as much as possible. Upon this principle it was, then, that he objected to their being allowed to take up any more of their Lordships' time; for what they proved, had nothing at all to do with the bill: as far as he could judge, what they were about to prove, was of as little consequence; they had already been indulged to a great length, and he had waited, expecting their own understanding would make them draw to a conclusion; instead of which, he perceived, the more they were indulged, the greater lengths they were determined to proceed. Those who meant to oppose the bill, he found, were resolved to protract it as long as possible: but he called upon their Lordships to remember the necessity of passing it immediately, if it was passed at all; for every gentleman knew, that to procure a quick passage to India, they must sail by the beginning of February at the farthest; we were now far advanced in December, and should it be much longer delayed, it would be impossible for gentlemen who might be appointed to go out, in consequence of another bill which was to be brought up to their Lordships, to get themselves ready in time. It appeared, as agreed on all hands, that some regulations ought to be adopted, and this appeared to him, as it had been framed with the greatest care and attention, as fully adequate to the task. Time pressed for its determination; and therefore he trusted, that these poor attempts to procrastinate the business, would be treated by their Lordships as they merited: in confidence of which, he doubted not they would restrain Counsel from entering into a large field of examination and investigation, that could not possibly tend to any other end than to delay and protract the reading of the bill. He therefore conjured their Lordships to restrict the evidence before them to the point to be agitated; and for this purpose he would move, that the Counsel at the bar be restrained from adducing the evidence of a peace being concluded in the Carnatic.

Lord Thurlow differed entirely with the learned Lord, respecting the evidence that had already been produced. He conceived the Counsel had acted with the greatest propriety; their clients had employed them, to do what? — only to rescue them from a general imputation laid against them in the bill, for it brought no specific charge. How was it possible for them to defend themselves, otherwise than by producing, in the first instance, authentic documents to their right, and afterwards, by a fair statement of their transactions and circumstances, to prove they had not abused that right. He agreed with the learned Lord, that some part of the evidence which had been produced at the bar might as well have been omitted; but he was far from saying, that held good with regard to the dispatches that were to prove that peace was established in India; and for this plain reason — the preamble of the bill stated, that by the mismanagement of the Company, they had brought themselves almost to a bankrupt state, and that it required

quired the immediate interpofition of Government to fave them from ruin. Now if they could adduce evidence to prove they had not mifmanaged, but that their finances here were not defpicable, and their fituation abroad in a flourifhing ftate, furely the preamble of the bill could not be founded in fact, and that plea of neceffity, which had been fo ftrenuoufly dwelt upon, did not exift, for then there could be no neceffity for this meafure. Ay, but then, fays the learned Lord, if the bill does not pafs immediately, which is folely for the regulation of the Company's affairs at home, it will totally prevent gentlemen from failing in proper time to take upon them their appointments in India. What advantage was intended by that argument, he was entirely at a lofs to comprehend: but even admitting the Company were actually the culprits they were faid to be, would their Lordfhips have it recorded in their Journals, that they had refufed to give them an opportunity to eftablifh their innocence? Should it be faid, that the conftitution of this country allowed an individual, where his property was concerned, to appear by counfel at the bar of that Houfe, and give his reafons why they fhould not proceed, and yet, when an act was brought in to deprive a corporate body of their charter, and to inveft their property in the hands of ftrangers, their Counfel fhould be checked, and reftrained from producing that evidence which, in all likelihood, would prove their affairs were in fo excellent a train, that it would not be in the power of mifmanagement, in the power of whoever this bill might appoint, to put them in diforder. If the learned Lord had thought the Counfel were guilty of mif-fpending their Lordfhips' time, why did he not ftate his fufpicions fooner? Why did he leave it till peace was mentioned, and proofs were offered of its being ratified, with the authorities, and that hoftilities were ceafed in the Carnatic? Thefe were circumftances that would not, moft certainly, act very forcibly in criminating the Company for mifmanagement, or for having brought them-

felves

selves on the verge of ruin; perhaps it was upon this principle they had been objected to. When parties were admitted to the bar of that House, their case would be peculiarly hard, if any noble Lord could get up and restrain the Counsel from what might very likely be the most material part of his evidence. Could such a measure be called justice? If not, should it be said, that the first court of judicature in this kingdom gave sanction to it? He trusted not. The people's rights ought to be held sacred; and it would be highly subversive of those rights, in his opinion, to punish where no delinquency was proved, to censure where every approbation was due. The business before your Lordships is of such a complicated and critical description, that every species of information will be found indispensable to a fair and candid apprehension of it. And instead of blaming Counsel for giving you too much, your Lordships ought to thank them for the pains they have taken to contract it into a proper form, and present it at your Lord-

Lordships' bar under a clear and connected point of view. They might, instead of a few papers, not tedious or complicated, they might have insisted on reading five hundred volumes: this, however, they have relinquished for such an abstract of the whole, as may not interfere either with the patience or the ordinary mode of the House. The learned Lord had dwelt much upon the idea, that it was a wish with some persons to protract the bill. Rumours may be propagated of such a nature and tendency, as to frustrate all the purposes of the bill. Who would have expected an observation of this sort from the noble and learned Lord? Ministry ought to be the last, at least, to hazard such surmises. Who knows not how industriously their creatures are occupied in this kind of work? For his part, he thought it of too much consequence to be passed hastily through that House. He could wish their Lordships to consider it as he did, as a bill of the utmost consequence and greatest importance; then would they exa-

examine minutely into every argument that could be adduced, and determine on facts, not on general implication. The papers, it was likewise said, were generally known; they were in every body's hands. This, to be sure, in a great measure, he could not deny; for he supposed their Lordships were as well acquainted how they came in every body's hands as he was: a gentleman had sent them to him, and he doubted not that very few of their Lordships had been omitted. It was, however, very singular to him, that the learned Lord, who certainly was an ornament to his profession, should object to papers as evidence, because they were printed; this was a new doctrine to him: but, however, the papers that were now offered, and were objected to, were not printed, they were not in every body's hands, for they had not long been received, therefore they certainly might be admitted without giving offence to the noble Lord on that head, and prove of some information to the House, as they would, perhaps; there did

not

not exist that pressing necessity for passing this bill, as had been held forth in another place: it is therefore hoped your Lordships will beware how you proceed. Violate not the rules of the House, in complaisance to a measure which originates in an open violation of whatever is most dear and sacred to Englishmen. Respect your own dignity, and the privilege of Parliament. Forms are the hedges of the constitution. The moment those are broken down, that is lost.

The Earl of Mansfield left the woolsack, and agreed with the noble Lord, whose objections to the course of evidence at the bar were now under discussion, that a very considerable part of that evidence had no immediate or obvious connection with the bill before the House. The present measure was a strong and severe one; and the stronger and more severe it was, the more were the Company entitled to struggle against it. To curtail or derange their evidence would, for that reason, have an appearance

pearance of harshness, which the prudence and delicacy of their Lordships would naturally dispose them to avoid. He did not see any disadvantage to the bill, if right, that could result from whatever facts might be suggested; and if it was ultimately found to be wrong, their Lordships' time could not have been better employed. But that which had been proposed, and which related to restoration of peace in the Carnatic, he conceived to be altogether in point; for the question on which the House was called to decide, would, in his Lordship's apprehension, be materially affected by that fact. He owned, however, that the bill deserved immediate investigation, and that too much dispatch could hardly be given to it, for the reasons the learned Lord had assigned: but his Lordship imagined, that much unnecessary delay would be occasioned by the present motion; he could therefore have wished his Lordship had not, on that account opposed it, and that the Counsel had been allowed to give them in his own way. What referred to the Carnatic, he presumed would

would not be long, as he apprehended it was only a letter from Lord Macartney afcertaining the perfect evacuation of that country.

Lord Loughborough had yet heard nothing to fatisfy him that his objection was not founded; and to him, time appeared juft now of infinite importance. This was only part of a plan for regulating the affairs of India. Should their Lordfhips approve the principle of it, and fanctify it by their adoption, a great many other bills would necefsarily follow. And it was proper to put their Lordfhips in mind, that a few weeks delay would prevent the effect of the meafure one whole year. The fhips for India muft be ready to fail fome time in February; and many things befides the mere pafsing of the bills were necefsary. With a view to that event, whatever the noble and learned Lord near him (Lord Thurlow) might think of rumours, he mentioned it as a fact, that a rumour was circulated, and had reached his ear fince he

came

came to that House, that the Counsel had been actually instructed and enjoined by their clients to protract the time by every possible manœuvre in their power. He therefore had deemed it his duty to apprize their Lordships of a circumstance which it became them to treat as it deserved. This objection, however, was founded on the nature of the bill, as independent alike of whatever might be the present state of India. This, though not affected by any thing yet advanced, he was willing, as far as his single voice went, to forego, and to give the Counsel whatever indulgence the House might think proper to grant them.

The Duke of Richmond was not disposed to consider that as an indulgence to which the subject had an undeniable right. And he wished noble Lords, in throwing out general things, would never suffer any language or phraseology to escape them, not strictly constitutional. In his opinion, the justice of the House, as well as the franchises of the subjects, was intimately connected with the question before their Lordships. And these, in his mind, were objects much more valuable than all India. What colour would this be to violate privileges, as fundamental and sacred as any which the laws provided? A Company are not only deprived of their property, but grossly calumniated. They came before this House abundantly prepared to have vindicated their rights, and in the very midst of their evidence are stopped, their Counsel deranged, and their defence consequently defeated. He therefore appealed to the justice and the dignity of the House in behalf of the Company and their rights.

Lord Thurlow was rather hurt by the boon which the noble and learned Lord held out to the Company by way of compromise. Neither did he rightly comprehend the expedition so strenuously urged on the occasion. The whole affair struck his Lordship rather ludicrously, as if it were the intention of Government to send out their new plan of Asiatic regulation by halves,

halves, in order that one part might serve only as a prologue to the other. It was indeed but too obvious, that a breach was meditated in the body of evidence, in order to throw the whole into confusion.

His Lordship took notice of a practice in the committee for trying the validity of elections, by which counsel were often intimidated and disconcerted in such a manner, as to render their best digested system of agitation abortive.

Lord Loughborough was certain, whatever the intention of the learned Lord near him might have been by these oblique observations, the good sense of the Counsel was a refutation of them. Though he wished them to act the part assigned them by the noble Lord, they were incapable of stooping to it. His Lordship had already waved the objection, though nothing had been urged to satisfy him of its invalidity; and he could not now trespass longer on their Lordships' time in answering any thing farther that might be suggested.

Lord

Lord Grantley (notwithstanding the learned Lord's sarcasm about the inattention of their Lordships) had not been absent during all the evidence which had been offered at the bar. He asserted his absolute independence of all parties, and was happy that his mind met the present business altogether unwarped by prejudice or connection of any kind. He did not, however, subscribe implicitly to the doctrine held out by the noble and learned Lord who had objected to the evidence at the bar. The relevancy of the evidence to the bill in question he thought very plain. The Company were charged with improper management. How could they otherwise proceed in their own vindication than by such a system of proof as their Counsel now offered to their consideration? The learned Lord tells the House that the paper respecting the recommencement of peace in the Carnatic is printed. What! Does the noble and learned Lord infer from that, our obligation to take all the lyes and falsehoods in circulation as facts because they may be printed? He must

muſt know better. This Houſe is not competent to receive any other than legal evidence.

The Earl of Effingham did not diſlike a protraction of the buſineſs, though he hoped the ſuſpicions of the learned Lord to that effect were nugatory and unfounded. He would not therefore conſume their Lordſhips time by practiſing the very thing he condemned. He had ſimply riſen to expreſs his approbation of the mode in which the Counſel at the bar had conducted the evidence, and to aſſure their Lordſhips that he watched for an opportunity when he might, conſiſtently with the order of the Houſe, move to poſtpone the whole matter till their Lordſhips had more thoroughly digeſted and matured it in their own minds.

The Counſel then went on with their evidence; but at half an hour after eleven o'clock the Counſel declared, that ſeveral of the witneſſes they wiſhed to have examined had gone off on account of the heat of the Houſe, not being held by proceſs; that
ſome

some of the books they wished to have submitted to the inspection of their Lordships, as essential to the cause, had been neglected to be brought up, and they therefore expressed a wish, that the farther prosecution of the business might be postponed to another day.

The Duke of Chandos, on this symptom of procrastination in the Counsel, rose, and moved an adjournment, urging, in favour of his motion, the extreme importance of the matter under consideration, and the lateness of the hour.

The Earl of Carlisle reprobated the idea of adjourning the farther hearing of the cause, for the frivolous reasons mentioned by the Counsel. Had not their Lordships met for the purpose of hearing the cause? Had they not bestowed on it every attention which it seemed to merit? Was it therefore becoming their dignity to desist procedure in the business at so important a period? Would this not be trifling with the

deference

deference and respect they owed themselves? He was therefore against the motion of adjournment.

Earl Fitzwilliam declared his disapprobation of the motion. He could not think there was the least pretence for the gentlemen at the Bar, to expect their application for farther time to prepare themselves, should meet with indulgence, since the petition, in support of which they had been heard so many hours, had been presented six days ago, and since the very same gentlemen had appeared at the Bar of the House of Commons, as advocates for a similar petition presented to that House against the same bill, his Lordship desired the House particularly to take notice of what had fallen from the learned Counsel in his opening, when he had told them that he had not received those instructions, in consequence of which he had proceeded to examine the witnesses produced that day, till eleven o'clock the preceding night, or eleven o'clock that very day. That declaration, the Earl faid, confirmed him in thofe fufpicions hinted at earlier in the day, that there was an intention to procraftinate and delay the bill as much as poffible, in order, by that means, to prevent its being paffed. He appealed to the Houfe in general, whether fo odd a circumftance as the neglecting to give Counfel inftructions in due time, againft a bill that had been for fome weeks before Parliament, did not carry with it a very fufpicious appearance? He hoped, therefore, the Houfe would render fruitlefs any fuch attempt, and that they would concur with him in directing the Counfel to proceed.

Earl Ferrers then rofe, and faid, my Lords, I am forry to be obliged to trouble your Lordfhips at this late hour, but the great regard I have for my King and the conftitution of this kingdom, forces me to ftand forth in its defence, and as a truly independent Lord of Parliament, being thoroughly fatisfied that if this bill paffes this Houfe, nobody can be fafe under the
exer-

exertions of the legiflative power, and particularly as there is one precedent to quote on this occafion, which is but a fmall one in comparifon with this, though it was a Lord of this Houfe (whofe eftate was above 5000l. a year) was taken from him and vefted in the hands of four truftees, with a power of leafing and cutting down the wood, with a receiver on his whole eftate, to pay an annuity of 300l. a year. I beg leave to fay farther, that I am totally againft hurrying bills through the Houfe, which can very rarely be done with any good defign; and we have an inftance in the laft year of what the public fuffered by hurrying the Receipt Tax through this Houfe, which I endeavoured to prevent, and would have informed the Miniftry what would be the confequence, if they would have permitted me, which would have prevented the people in all the manufacturing towns, long tormented with fuch a vexatious tax, befide the difcredit it has been to the Minifter, which I would have faved him from. I am, therefore, for giving a bill of this magnitude and

con-

confequence, its full weight and confideration; and for that reason shall join most heartily in the motion for an adjournment.

Lord Sidney alfo faid, the bill was of too much importance to be hurried; and declared before their Lordships paffed fuch a bill, they were bound to hear the petitioners in the ampleft manner.

The Duke of Chandos rofe again, and declared he addreffed himfelf to the feelings of the Houfe, begging their Lordships would confider, whether, after the learned gentlemen had been on their legs at the Bar, for feven hours, incommoded by the croud around them, and fatigued with the heat they all felt, and after they had requefted till the next morning only to prepare themfelves, it was confiftent with their own character, and their own dignity, to infift on their proceeding, efpecially at fo late an hour of the night?

The Duke of Portland faid, he fhould willingly have agreed to the motion propofed posed by the noble Duke, and have acceeded to the requisition of the Counsel, had there appeared to him to have been the smallest reason to justify the latter. But as the bill had been in Parliament for some weeks, as it proposed a measure that had been much canvassed and talked of, and as that measure was of very considerable importance, and from its nature, and the nature of the subject to which it applied, such as ought, if adopted by the wisdom of their Lordships, to be adopted with as little delay as the forms of Parliament would admit, he could by no means give his consent to the motion. Being upon his legs, the Duke said, he would mention a matter, to which he begged their Lordships' most serious attention, since it materially concerned the constitution of the country: a rumour had prevailed for the last three days, that had given him very great alarm indeed; so much alarm, that he had determined to state it to their Lordships on the very first day that they met after it began to be circulated; and he should, he said, have done it much

much earlier in the day, but that he was loath to break through the regularity of their proceedings, or draw off the attention of the House from hearing Counsel against a bill, which certainly was of great importance. Since that bill had been brought into Parliament, the public had been inflamed against it in the most industrious, and, in some degree, most successful manner. No arts, however unfair, however unwarrantable, had been left untried to run it down, and excite a general alarm, in consequence of a gross misrepresentation of its views and its object. Among other arts, rumours of different kinds had been circulated with the most sedulous industry, and a late rumour was of a very extraordinary nature indeed. In that rumour, the name of the most sacred character in the kingdom had been aspersed, and the name of one of their Lordships, he hoped, abused; but certainly, such was the complection of the rumour, that he should be wanting in regard to his own character, wanting in that love and zeal for the constitution, which, he trusted,

had

had ever marked and diſtinguiſhed his political life, wanting in the duty he owed to the public as a Miniſter, if he did not take an opportunity, if it turned out to be true, of propoſing a meaſure upon it to their Lordſhips, that would prove they felt the ſame jealouſy, the ſame deteſtation, and the ſame deſire to mark and ſtigmatize every attempt to violate the conſtitution, as he did.

The Duke of Richmond roſe, and declared, that from the hint the noble Duke had thrown out, it was impoſſible to ſay to what he alluded. In a matter of ſo much ſeriouſneſs, he ought to ſpeak out, and to make a ſpecific charge, that thoſe it might affect, ſhould be able to meet it fairly, and bring it to a plain and direct iſſue. The noble Duke might allude to one thing, or he might allude to ſomething elſe extremely different, which was at that time in his recollection. A newſpaper, which he had in his pocket, his Grace ſaid, contained as indecent and as ſcandalous a paragraph, as ever he had met with; perhaps the noble
Duke

Duke alluded to the fact there stated. He would read it to the House. His grace then read the following article from an evening paper of Saturday:

"A most injurious and absurd rumour
"prevailed yesterday, and was circulated
"with great industry through the various
"parts of the metropolis, that his Maje-
"sty had given a direct intimation to his
"Ministers that he was hostile to the East-
"India bill, and that they in consequence
"had resigned their respective employ-
"ments.—We have the best authority for
"assuring our readers that no part of this
"report is true. To give a greater air of
"credibility to the falsehood, it was repre-
"sented that this event had taken place in
"consequence of a conference that Earl
"Temple had held with his Majesty on
"Thursday last, the result of which was
"said to have been a positive assurance on
"the part of the King, that the bill in
"question was in the highest degree disa-
"greeable to him. This concomitant part

" of the story, however, is an evident and
" indisputable libel upon the characters of
" both these great personages concerned in
" it; for we can assure our readers, (also
" from the best authority) that his Maje-
" sty has given his gracious concurrence
" and approbation of the conduct of his
" Ministers, with respect to the India bill,
" a thousand times in the closet, nay, in-
" deed, as often as it has been mentioned
" there. Now to suppose or impute to any
" man, much less to this sacred character,
" so despicable a degree of confirmed dupli-
" city as that of his having approved and
" patronised a measure in all the stages of
" its progress, from its first adoption till its
" third reading in the House of Commons,
" and yet that he was in fact averse to it, is
" too gross for belief, and is in this instance
" an act of the highest disloyalty. That
" Lord Temple should have circulated such
" a report, knowing it, as he must, to have
" been founded in direct falsehood, is not
" extremely probable; and therefore the
" whole must, doubtless, have been the im-
" pudent

" pudent fabrication of some hired runner,
" to produce a temporary alarm in the me-
" tropolis, and to try to effect by tumult,
" what they could not carry by argu-
" ment."

The above, his Grace said, was as extraordinary a series of assertions, declared to come from the best authority, as ever occurred in a newspaper.

Earl Temple rose as soon as the Duke sat down, and said, conscious as he was that every word he must utter would be entirely unparliamentary; yet, after what had been suggested by the noble Duke who spoke first, and after his name had been introduced by the noble Duke who spoke last, though he must think, not in the most parliamentary way, he should persist in desiring to be heard. The noble Duke at the head of the Treasury talked of rumours; let the noble Duke make a specific charge. Whenever he did so, he would not shrink from it, but would meet it directly. That
his

his Majesty had recently honoured him with a conference, was a matter of notoriety. It was not what he wished to deny, nor what he had it in his power to conceal. He said, that it was the privilege of Peers, as the hereditary counsellors of the Crown, either individually or collectively, to advise the Crown, was well known. He had given his advice to the Crown; what that advice had been, he would not then say. It was lodged in the breast of his Majesty; nor would he declare the purport of it without the royal consent, or till he saw a proper occasion. He was aware this sort of language was disorderly; he begged the House however to recollect that he had not made it necessary; if Lord Temple's name had been introduced, it had not been the fault of Lord Temple. When the noble Duke mentioned rumours, and did not specify to what he alluded, he had been silent; and he should have continued in silence, and have treated every thing of that sort with the same contempt that he held newspaper paragraphs in, had not the noble Duke, who spoke last, made it impossible for him not to rise, and defy the noble Duke at the head of the Treasury to make any charge that he would shrink from. He begged to know therefore what the noble Duke had alluded to?

The Duke of Richmond rose again, and said, perhaps he had been disorderly in reading the paragraph from the newspaper; but the noble Duke who talked of rumours had done it in a manner so general and indefinite, that he had thought it highly necessary to have the matter explained and understood. If the noble Duke meant to take up all unconstitutional interference with the Crown, he would join him, and go as far with him upon that theme as he would go himself; but then the noble Duke must go back to his old ground, and leave his present connections. He must once more act as a Whig, and proceed upon Whig principles. He hoped, however, when the noble Duke did take up that matter, he would take it up fairly, and not partially.

partially. That he would look at home, and draw forth all unconstitutional interference with the Crown, that of Ministers, as well as that of other Lords. He knew, the Duke said, that it was the duty of the servants of the Crown to be about the King's person, and to consult and advise with his Majesty upon the receipt of foreign advices, upon the management of his finances, upon the conduct of the Army or Navy, upon military and civil promotions, and a variety of other executive subjects, in which his Majesty was necessarily to be consulted; but he would contend it was as unconstitutional for a Minister to advise the Crown, and endeavour to influence his Majesty in regard to any bill depending in Parliament, as it was for any other person. The present Administration, he asserted, had, from their first coming in, proceeded to act in defiance of Whig principles, and upon the old system, pursued by those whom they formerly opposed. They had manifestly taken unconstitutional ground, and governed by a corrupt influence. When they

they firſt came in, they had aſked, the Duke ſaid, if he would join them. Though he liked many in Adminiſtration, he declared he could not aſſiſt ſuch an Adminiſtration; he foreſaw what would follow, and his expectation had not been diſappointed. The bill then before the Houſe was a proof of the ſort of ſyſtem which Miniſters had laid down. As he could not join them, he had quitted his ſituation, and left the Ordnance. What was the conſequence? —Three gentlemen, with no political views, nor in any way connected with influence, whom he had brought into office, were turned out, and three members of Parliament introduced. Another inſtance he would adduce; and that was, the giving Sir William Gordon, a gentleman who had ſerved as an Ambaſſador abroad, a penſion of 1000l. a year. What could this be for, but to give up his ſeat in Parliament, that they might bring in a new member for Portſmouth? A very able member indeed, Mr. Erſkine. The Duke expatiated upon theſe two facts, and urged them

them as proofs that the prefent Adminiftration went entirely upon a fyftem of corrupt influence.

The Earl of Derby begged the noble Duke to look at home himfelf, before he ventured to impute blame to others. When the noble Duke was at the head of the Ordnance, he brought his friends into office, as other men in high ftations generally did; and it was notorious that two, if not more of thofe friends, were in Parliament. His Lordfhip took notice of the rumours abroad for the laft three days, and reprobated fuch unconftitutional means of endeavouring to fubvert a bill, which could not be overthrown by fair argument.

The Duke of Richmond rofe again, and in order to juftify himfelf, went into a detail of his conduct when in office. He faid, he had brought into the Ordnance Mr. Crawfurd, Mr. Aldridge, and Mr. Smyth, neither of them in Parliament, in the room of Sir Charles Cocks, Mr. Strachey

chey, and Mr. Adam, all of whom were in Parliament; that Mr. Pelham, who had succeeded Sir Charles Frederick as Surveyor General, was in Parliament, and Mr. Steele, who was his private Secretary. Much as he disliked influence, the Duke said, and greatly as he had approved a place bill, it had always been a maxim with him, and which had often been declared by him, that one or two gentlemen belonging to each public office, ought to be in the House of Commons. In his own case, he had but two of his official connections in that House, viz. Mr. Pelham for the Board, and Mr. Steele for himself. He said farther, that he had, on many occasions, stood up for the liberties of the people; he had also, when occasion required, defended the privileges of that House; and he should be equally ready to contend for the constitutional prerogative of the Crown, whenever it was attempted to be invaded, as it was, he contended, most violently by the bill then under consideration.

Earl

Earl Temple rose again, and said, as the noble Duke in his eye had not thought proper to make any reply to his question, he begged their Lordships to hold it in mind, that the noble Duke had said in his former speech, that he did not charge him with having acted in the unconstitutional manner, the rumours and the newspaper paragraphs had dared to state. It was necessary that it should be so understood. What the advice was, that he had given his Majesty, it was not then necessary for him to recite; but when his Majesty should give him permission to divulge it, he should venture to assure their Lordships, that it would be found to be the advice of an honest man. With regard to the matter before them, the consideration, whether the Counsel, who had declared they begged to be indulged till morning, should be ordered to proceed or not, their Lordships would determine as they thought proper. He was a young man, capable of continuing there as long as any one of them; but their Lordships ought to consider, that they

they had those among them not quite so young, nor so fit to endure fatigue. The bill in every point of view was such a bill as ought not to be hurried. From the evidence that had been laid before them that day, it was evident that it was a direct violation of the rights and franchises of the East-India Company, rights and franchises vested in them by a great variety of charters and acts of Parliament. This was a consideration that must come home to the bosom of every Englishman, and was sufficiently important to justify the most serious deliberation; but there was another consideration still more important, and that was, the new and unconstitutional power it would create. This his Lordship enlarged upon as a matter which called for the most scrupulous care on the part of the House; he concluded, therefore, with hoping they would adjourn, in order to give the Counsel an opportunity of proceeding with the rest of their evidence in the morning.

The

The Duke of Portland rose again, and said, he had not in his former speech made any charge against the noble Earl, nor did he then mean to make any specific charge. The rumours he had before alluded to, had given him very serious alarm, because they spoke confidently of a mode of interference having been practised, with a view to defeat the bill, unknown to the constitution, and which had not been heard of in that country, at least not for a long time. But he begged leave to assure the noble Earl, that he did not take up the rumour from a newspaper; he had not known it had got into the newspapers, till the noble Duke produced that, which he had read the paragraph from a little before. The rumours had been notorious, and not confined to any particular set of individuals, but had been in every body's mouth, all over the town, for the last three or four days. The facts asserted in those rumours, if proved, were of a most serious nature, and such as would, in that case, make it necessary for him to ground a proposition to their Lordships upon, in which he had no manner of doubt but the whole House would go along with him.

Lord Viscount Townshend said, he had wished to say a few words, if it were only for the purpose of calling their Lordships' attention back again to the subject, that had first given rise to the debate, which had taken so extraordinary a turn. It was, whether the Counsel at the bar should be indulged till the next morning to prepare themselves farther, or should be ordered to proceed in the best manner they could then? This question had been started an hour since; so that out of compassion to the two learned gentlemen, who desired to proceed no farther, that House had gone into a debate, and kept them standing at the bar a full hour, as little regarded as a couple of hackney coach-horses standing at an ale-house door. The request of the two learned gentlemen, his Lordship said, if complied with, he hoped was not meant as a beginning of more procrastination than
that

that of a single day. He had not yet heard any thing against the bill that had induced him to think upon it in any other light, than that in which the noble Duke at the head of the Treasury had placed it. But he was certain, if it passed at all, it was necessary to pass with dispatch. The season required it. Every body knew that it could not be sent out to India so as to take effect there early, unless it went in February; there was an end of any reformation in India, therefore, for another year, should it not be sent out in that month; and it was for this reason, without meaning to give offence to any individual Lords, that he earnestly hoped no management, no endeavours to occasion delay, would be practised. His Lordship repeated what he had said on Tuesday last, that he never saw a bill more deliberately, nor more carefully conducted through a Committee, than this bill had been conducted through the Committee of the House of Commons. Every objection had been listened to, and every reasonable alteration adopted. He
wished,

wished, therefore, as little delay as possible might now attend it. With regard to what a noble Duke, his successor and his predecessor in office, had said about influence, he was a little surprized. That noble Duke, upon a coalition having been formed before that, now so much condemned, and which had proved far more unpleasant to him, had been made Master General of the Ordnance. The noble Duke then put his own friends into office. Nobody blamed him for it; but if influence was to be talked of, what had turned his friends Mr. Strachey, Mr. Adam, and others out? Nothing but influence. Every man at the head of an office naturally liked to have those about him, in whom he placed confidence. For this reason it was, that when he came in again he brought back his old friends. The Ordnance had been called an Augean stable. The noble Duke had set about cleansing it, and he thought his friends could best assist his labours. He in like manner chose to trust his, because he thought they could remove

move the dirt away as faſt as any other people. But, to return to the queſtion, he wiſhed their Lordſhips would relieve the gentlemen at the bar ———

Earl Fitzwilliam ſaid, he was glad the noble Duke had mentioned the rumours that had lately prevailed, ſince it had afforded the noble Earl ſo fair an opportunity of anſwering, and declaring them falſe.

Earl Temple deſired the noble Earl not to miſunderſtand him. He had given no anſwer either one way or the other, nor would he give any anſwer, till a plain, direct, and ſpecific charge was urged: That he would meet without ſhrinking; but he would only treat rumours and newſpaper libels with contempt.

Earl Fitzwilliam again urged it to the Houſe, that the Counſel's declaration of his not having received his inſtructions till eleven o'clock the preceding evening, although

though so much time had elapsed since the contents of the bill were known, very forcibly impressed his mind with a suspicion, that a plan of procrastination and affected delay was adopted with a view to defeat the bill's success. He therefore declared, he could not consent to the motion of adjournment. With regard to the assertion of a noble Duke, that the Minister who should advise the Crown to support a bill depending in Parliament, and endavour to influence the Crown in its favour, would act unconstitutionally, he denied the doctrine. If he knew any thing of the British constitution, the reverse was the fact. The Crown could do no wrong. The Minister alone was responsible for every measure of government, while he was in office. He had a right, therefore, constitutionally, to exert his influence with the Crown, and indeed it would be impossible for any government to go on without such exertion. The case was widely different, as the rumour stated the facts, to which the noble Duke had alluded, when he spoke of the alarm,

alarm, which the rumour that prevailed univerfally for the three laſt days had occafioned. The rumour confidently faid, that the noble Earl in his eye had advifed his Majefty againſt ——

Earl Temple rofe immediately, and defired that the noble Earl's words might be taken down.

The Earl of Carlifle reminded their Lordfhips, that according to the order of the Houfe, when any noble Lord's words were moved to be taken down, the bar muſt be cleared.

Strangers were upon this ordered to withdraw.

While they were out, as Earl Fitzwilliam merely ſtated the facts alledged againſt Earl Temple as matter of rumour, Earl Temple begged pardon for having given their Lordfhips fo much trouble, and waved his requeſt of having the words taken down.

The queftion of adjournment was then put, and the Houfe divided.

| Contents | - | 69 | Not contents | 57 |
| Proxies | - - | 18 | Proxies | - - | 22 |

              87   79
Majority for the adjournment   8

WEDNESDAY, *December* 17.

In purfuance of the order of the day the Lords were fummoned on the fecond reading of the bill for better regulating the affairs of the Eaft-India Company, &c. which being read,

Earl Gower rofe, and obferved, that, from the bill itfelf, and from what he had heard fo clearly, ably, and diftinctly urged at the bar, he could not refift the impulfe of declaring his diffent to the bill. He felt it fo forcibly, that he fhould not be fatisfied with giving it a filent negative—it
went

went to condemn where no criminality was proved—it went to rob a body of men of their corporate rights, without the appearance of guilt, nay, when their innocence was clearly established. It had been called a bold and rapid measure; it was a bold one he would admit, for, as it appeared to him, it militated against the constitution of this country—he was happy to see it was considered as of the greatest consequence by many noble Lords, as well as himself, and had brought them, as it had done him, from their country retirements. He had not thought of coming to town until he received a copy of this bill, which he no sooner read, than its alarming tendency made him determine to set off and give what weight he possibly could towards its rejection—that House had proceeded with the most tenacious precaution when a body of people were to be deprived of their franchises in another case, and were satisfied of their delinquency before they would give their sanction and assent to such a measure; had any delinqency been proved, had any been attempted, by which thefe men had forfeited their chartered rights? Certainly not. It was said they are bankrupts. Was that the fact? Had not the contrary been clearly adduced, from authentic papers, documents, and ftatements which they had produced in their own behalf, and were now upon their Lordfhips' table? He would, however, ftate what appeared to him the pretended and the real caufe for this bill. It was once pretended, that from the circumftances of the Company, the mifmanagement of their Directors, and the difobedience of their fervants abroad, actual ruin ftared them in the face, and made a neceffity for Parliament to interfere, to fave them from ruin. The real caufe, he fufpected, was the amazing patronage that would be acquired to the Minifter by this new arrangement. There might be a neceffity for keeping the prefent Adminiftration upon folid grounds, without the apprehenfion of being removed; and the influence that would undoubtedly be acquired by this meafure under that confideration,

ation, was very far from being contemptible: but was that sufficient for their Lordships to consent to a violation of charter, to the seizure of property, and the annihilation of a Company which had maintained its credit as the first commercial Company in the world for upwards of two centuries? Surely not. They would be convinced, that the necessity for this violent measure did actually exist, before they would adopt it. If the bill should pass, which he trusted would never be the case, and the influence that it would really throw into the hands of the Minister was considered, he conceived that the title with propriety might be altered to, An Act for regulating the East-India Company, for the better Government of Great Britain.

The Earl of Carlisle declared, that if he could agree in any point which had fallen from his noble relation, it was in the able manner in which the Counsel at their Lordships' bar had stood forth in the cause of their employers; but at the same time he entreated

treated the House would recollect, they had heard only one side of the question, and that the cause must be bad, indeed, which those learned gentlemen could not put a tolerable face upon, especially when there was no person to contradict what they asserted. The bill, in his opinion, was highly necessary; and he had not drawn his opinion from mere assertions only, but from the actual state of the Company's affairs: their debt was enormous, and the account they had made out was fallacious and erroneous in the highest degree, as he would prove to their Lordships—in the first instance, they had charged Government with a debt of 4,200,000l. which was by no means a fair estimate, because this was not due from Government while the Company held the monopoly of trade, and there was not, at present, the least intention of taking that monopoly from them. Allowing, however, that they had a right to state in the account of their property what was due from Government, that money being sunk in the three per cents, if the Company

chose

chose to call for it, without Government's interference with their monopoly, they certainly had no right to estimate the debt at any higher rate than the price of the funds in which that property was vested; he should therefore make a deduction in the first article of the credit side of their account, of 1,680,000 pounds, which would reduce it to 2,520,000 pounds. The like objections were applicable to the greatest part of the estimate they had produced, as a vindication of their flourishing state. His Lordship then read the various statements, and made nearly the same objections to them as Mr. Fox had done in the House of Commons; and concluded these observations by remarking, that the Company, instead of having a balance of upwards of 3,000,000l. they were above 6,000,000l. in arrears. This situation of their finances was not the only necessity for the interference of Parliament: the proceedings of their servants abroad, who paid little or no attention to the orders of the Court of Directors, were truly alarming; they

they were guilty of the moſt violent outrages, making peace or war as beſt ſuited their own intereſt; breaking treaties and leagues with the different Princes; ſweeping the inhabitants from the face of the earth, and committing ravages and enormities, that were not only a diſgrace to the Britiſh name, but to humanity: from the inability of the Directors, which had been plainly proved; for when they had determined on the removal of one of their ſervants, the Proprietors met, overturned that determination, and voted him their thanks for his conduct, although he had proceeded in open oppoſition to the orders he had received. It was plain, therefore, ſome regulations were neceſſary, if we wiſhed to keep thoſe territories; and theſe regulations, he was firmly of opinion, would be found in the bill before the Houſe, and would fully anſwer the purpoſe, if it was permitted to paſs. The Court of Directors might contain many worthy members; but he did not perceive, that it fell within the capacity of twenty-four merchants to

manage

manage with propriety the politics of so large a territory; they might act to the best of their judgment, but we had glaring proofs they did not always act right; and when they did, their orders were not paid the least attention to. It had been urged, that the Company by this bill was to be deprived of their property: but he would not admit that any such thing was to be the case; it was rather the contrary; their property being now in a precarious situation, Government offered their assistance to take care of it for them: but what was this property? It was not the property of an individual; it was a property in which the Public had as great, if not a much greater stake than the Company; and therefore, surely the Public, without any unconstitutional principle, had a right to interfere and take possession of that property, if they saw it mismanaged and in danger of being annihilated; he did not say so much by mismanagement at home, as by unwarrantable proceedings in India. He did not mean to criminate any man in particular by these charges; they were not confined to any one; rapacity and disobedience many were accountable for: but this regulation was rather intended to amend than criminate, to prevent future delinquency than to accuse for past. The violation of charters had also been much dwelt upon; but, according to his ideas, the State had an undoubted right to make alterations in those charters with which its interest was so intimately connected. The charter of the India Company was nothing more than a mutual agreement between them and the Public for both their advantages; they were to have a monopoly of the trade, to the exclusion of the rest of his Majesty's subjects; that monopoly it was still intended they should possess; and therefore he did not see their charter was to be violated in the least instance. For these, among a variety of other reasons, he had been induced to conceive the bill before the House as a measure that ought to be adopted, because it promised a redress of the evils that had long subsisted, a benefit to the advantages

tages arising from our commercial intercourse, and a permanency and stability to the maintenance of our territorial possessions in that country.

The Earl of Coventry wished to call their Lordships' attention to the dangerous innovation they were about to adopt; that of depriving a set of British subjects of their dearest rights, their franchises, and their property. If they were robbed of their charter, they lost their all. If charters were set at nought, there was an end of liberty. Did we not hold our freedom under Magna Charta? and was that of so trifling a nature, that it was to be treated as nothing? This measure appeared as a circumstance of alarm to all corporate bodies. Who would say, that Ministers might not next year think it adviseable to put the direction of the Bank into commission?—Might not the African Company expect it?—or, perhaps, they might choose to appoint in future, the Mayor of the city of London. These were conclusions he thought

thought every corporate body in the kingdom had a right to draw, provided the prefent bill was not checked in its career by their Lordfhips. He was fo far convinced in his own idea, that it was an infringement of the rights and liberties of the fubjects of this conftitution, that he would move it fhould be rejected.

The Duke of Manchefter was in favour of the bill; he was fo fatisfied of its neceffity, that he was refolved to give it his moft hearty fupport. He believed the Company in their ftatement had fet forth many articles that never would be forthcoming — He would not fay, that due from the Court of France for French prifoners was of a defperate kind; but he feared the receipt was not fo very certain, for when he had preffed for it, they had made a claim of a large fum for damages done by the India Company by filling up the ditch at Chenadogore. He did not mean to condemn this meafure; it might be defenfible in politics, although they had no right
what-

whatever for such a proceeding, and it admitted an argument against the demand of the India Company. The French Court had not omitted taking that advantage, and therefore he did not think it ought to be stated as cash in hand; our situation in India, he was clear, made it very requisite for some such regulation as was proposed by the bill; and unless that, or something of equal propriety, took place, would be found to lie in the utmost danger.

Lord Rawdon begged the indulgence of the House while he should give his sentiments upon the bill; he would not consider it in the many points of view in which it had been so often held up; with respect to the bankruptcy of the Company, the necessity or pressing occasion for passing it, but merely confine himself to the single point of its policy; he would not contend that there had not been great rapacity committed by the servants of the Company in India, and that some regulations were not very much wanted; but he would contend, this
bill

bill would not be productive of these requisite regulations; it would rather be productive of an influence in this country which no Minister ought to be intrusted with. Did their Lordships consider what the patronage of India was? this patronage was to be vested in the hands of seven gentlemen, who, it was natural to suppose were the friends of the Minister, and therefore the patronage was ultimately in him; if so, it was an influence too great for any Minister to be trusted with; and if he should go out of office, any other administration would be but a shadow against him. That great boast of English liberty, the guardians of the people, the House of Commons, he found would no longer be an independent body, but would contain a corrupt, and influenced majority. This he thought a sufficient reason for their Lordships to assume their dignity, and reject a bill that had such an apprehensive prospect for its tendency.—His objection to it arose not from party motives; he wished not for any such connection; but, from the principle of the

bill

bill itself, and that such a bill, fraught with such influence, should meet with support in noble Lords who had stood forth its advocates, was to him very surprising; one of them, the noble Lord at the head of the Treasury, of whom he had the highest opinion, nor was his veneration for the character of another noble Lord, who filled a high office in administration, less; that they should give sanction to a measure which was palpably the measure of a Minister; and for what purpose?—If their Lordships saw it in the same point of view he did, they would, like him, execrate it. He trusted, therefore, for their own honour, for the purity of the constitution, and rights and privileges of the people at large, the House would join with him in giving the commitment of the bill a negative.

Lord Sandwich paid many compliments to the last noble Lord, for the candour in which he had so ably descanted on the bill; but at the same time observed he was from principle, in many points obliged to differ from

from him; he did not perceive the ill consequences which the noble Lord apprehended, and he was thoroughly satisfied of the necessity for doing something speedily for the salvation of the Company. The noble Lord had admitted there were scenes of rapacity committed in India, which called aloud for a check; the Directors had been found, by experience, inadequate to the task; their orders were disregarded, and their commands held for nothing: he would give their Lordships, a particular instance—it happened that one of the Princes, by the death of his father, came to the government of his dominions while a minor; being in friendship with the Company, they thought they could not do less than, as his protector and friend, to see to his education; for this purpose the Directors sent over, that one of the most able and best masters should be procured for his instruction; and the servants to whom these orders went, obeyed these orders; but how, and who, and what was this well-instructed teacher?—Would your Lordships believe it, they actually put
him

him under the care of an old woman; nay, this was not all, but the moſt improper old woman in the country—they paſſed over his own, and put him under the care of his ſtep-mother—did not this appear as a plain mockery of the orders they received? He by no means objected to this tutor, becauſe ſhe was a female, for he was aware, and the experience of many of their Lordſhips could prove, that the inſtructions and aſſiſtance of females was of the greateſt ſervice, but then it was females who had received an European education, and not one who had been taken from a ſeraglio, and in a country where they are not allowed to think of a future ſtate; this however was thought a ſufficient inſtruction for the young Prince, or rather, as it appeared to him, done in direct oppoſition to the Directors. Was not this ſufficient to ſhew their Lordſhips how inadequate the Court of Directors were to the taſk of conducting and enforcing regulations for the advantage of the Company? He had no particular objection to any one of theſe Directors; and yet he muſt

R obſerve

observe, that no great things ought to be expected from them, if it was but recollected from what a motley groupe they were elected, men, women, children, young and old, foreigners, Jews, Papists, and Protestants; together with the interests of the different servants in India, whose friends were so numerous, as to render these gentlemen here, more their constituents than their masters; no wonder then so little attention was paid to their direction. Those who had objected to this bill had argued a great deal on the state of their property: he would not say they were bankrupts, but they had done that, which if any individual merchant had committed, he would have been looked upon as a bankrupt. Bills had become due, and they had not wherewithal to pay them. They had called their creditors together, and asked for time; with respect to taking their property, and vesting it in other hands, it was no more than would happen in private life; their affairs were in that situation to make them apply to their friends for assistance, and they had produced to the

persons

persons agreeable to lend them assistance, a statement of their accounts; on the examination of which, the friends still are willing to give that assistance, but observe your property is greatly mortgaged, your circumstances are greatly mismanaged: we will extricate you if possible, yet lest we should be involved in ruin with you, we will appoint persons that can he trusted to have the care of the property; this is the plain case; the public are those friends, and, doubtless ought to have some security for their trust. His Lordship dwelt for a considerable time on the enormities committed abroad, defended the bill in a most able manner, and concluded by recommending it as worthy the approbation of the House.

The Duke of Richmond and Lord Walsingham rose together: His Grace begged to be heard first, because he was anxious to say a few words, and he was sure from the very valuable fund of information which the noble Lord possessed upon the subject of India, he should have no chance of being attended to by their Lordſhips, if the noble Lord was to ſpeak before him. He ſaid, the Houſe was to be determined by the arguments and proofs, and not by the declamation of Counſel, a term which had been uſed by the noble Duke who ſpoke before him. That they had proved the affairs of the Company to be far from that ruinous ſtate in which they were repreſented to be. That, after perſonal liberty, private property was firſt under the protection of the law. If the Company have committed acts that warrant a forfeiture of their charter, why not try them before a Court of Judicature? If they are guilty of criminal offences, let them be arraigned as criminals. The interference of the Legiſlature, he inſiſted, was, in ſuch caſe, an infraction of liberty; and though ſome caſes might warrant the interference of the Legiſlature, yet that this was not one of that nature. The Company's charter had been renewed only two years back; gentlemen had purchaſed that ſtock, relying upon that charter.

He

He had often heard it urged as an argument against equalizing the land-tax, that estates had been purchased under a confidence that the Legislature would not equalize it. Would not this argument apply more strongly to the present case of the Proprietors of India Stock, who had purchased under the confidence that Government would not abrogate or annul a Charter, which was only two years since solemnly renewed. This bill, his Grace observed, was supposed by some noble Lords to be intended merely to increase the power of a certain Secretary, for whom, notwithstanding his difference with him in politics, he had a most sincere friendship and esteem. [Here the Duke made some handsome encomiums on his honourable relation, which it is needless for us to report minutely]; but however this bill might tend to increase the influence of an individual, his principal objection to it, considered in this light, arose from the dangerous innovation it made in the constitution, by confounding the powers of Government, and by giving to a

branch

branch of the legiflative a part of the executive power. That this bill placed the government of India in the hands of the Commons, and their Lordfhips need only recur to Holland to remark, how improper a democratic affembly is to manage the execution of public affairs. He was againft the bill going into a Committee, where a noble Duke, who had fpoken before him, faid, it might be fo altered and modified, as to meet with the concurrence of the Houfe; but, he urged, that no amendments or alterations could be effected to rectify what was in itfelf wrong *ab initio*: that he did not approve of the general principle: a vaft continent in India was to be governed by feven Commiffioners, refident in Britain, who were to tranfmit their orders to officers appointed in India, to carry them into execution. But he appealed to their Lordfhips, if orders, which were exceedingly proper at the moment they were given, might not be highly the reverfe at the moment of execution. No orders were,

in

in fact, to be implicitly obeyed; and on every trial for disobedience of orders it has always been enquired, whether such disobedience of orders was necessary or not. He needed not to remind their Lordships of a recent transaction at Saratoga. Here it was disputed, and remains to this moment a doubt, whether General Burgoyne's orders were peremptory or discretional. Besides, he saw nothing in the bill by which the new Commissioners were invested with powers superior to those of the old Directors; nor did he see why the power invested in the Commissioners, might not as well be confided to the Directors. The evidence, his Grace contended, was partial and insufficient, and that it was absurd to imagine that their Lordships could derive an adequate information from a few papers laid upon the table, by a member who was professedly an advocate for the bill. If a full and sufficient investigation of the Company's affairs be required, and without such full investigation it would be the heighth

of

of injuftice to deprive them of their property, and annihilate their charter; why not commit it to feven or eight members of the Houfe?—to a fmall committee—before which alone, and not before the whole Houfe, fo complicated a detail could be examined and enquired into with effect. To excufe the violation of the Company's property, it had been urged, that there are two kinds of property; one pofitive, and the other qualified, in which the public had a fhare or were interefted. But, his Grace maintained, that there is no property in the kindom but what the public has fome intereft in; as it is only of the aggregate poffeffions of individuals, that the public property confifts. He infifted, that the Counfel had laid a juft, exact ftatement of the Company's property before their Lordfhips; and in the objections that had been ftated to it, by a noble Lord, who fpoke, laft, he could have wifhed that one circumftance had been omitted, viz. the mention of the improbability of recovering a debt from the Court of France; and he could

not

not but think it improper and impolitic in the noble Duke to introduce it, though he knew not but the noble Duke might be authorised by his instructions to do it, whilst a negociation, relative to that very demand, was pending; for it could not be imagined but that the French Ministry would take the advantage of the Ambassador's declaration, and in consequence of what he said, be still more inclined to dispute the Company's demand, and with-hold the payment of it.

This called up the Duke of Manchester, who said, he should be happy to meet the noble Lord who spoke last; and after communicating to him his instructions, convince him that he had neither been guilty of imprudence or impolicy, in what he had said relative to the demand made by the East-India Company on the Court of France. He had only urged it as a fallacious statement, to set down as cash, what was still a matter of litigation; and, to say the best of it, doubtful in the issue.

The Duke of Richmond, in reply, said, all he meant was to insinuate the impolicy of touching on a matter in that House, from the discussion of which, an advantage might, and most probably would, be taken by the adversary.

The Duke of Manchester rose once more, and delared, that he had divulged nothing that ought to be kept secret, or that could give the Court of France any advantage in the discussion of the article alluded to.

Lord Walsingham observed, that after the very flattering distinction, and the very undeserved compliments that had been bestowed upon him by the noble Duke in the blue ribband, their Lordships might be led to expect an ampler discussion of the subject before them than he was able to give it; it would certainly, therefore, be necessary for him to apologize to their Lordships for the very imperfect manner in which he should deliver his sentiments upon the most important subject that, perhaps,

haps, had ever engaged their Lordships' attention. The bill then before the House was a bill which certainly took away from the proprietors of East-India stock, all management or interference in their own affairs. It tended, undoubtedly, to depreciate the value of their stock; because every proprietor of that Company had certainly a right to consider the share of patronage, which he heretofore enjoyed, as a part of the rights and privileges to which he was entitled, and that no lawful advantage, which the possession of his stock gave him, was to be forfeited, without delinquency fully proved against the East-India Company. Having stated this very fully, his Lordship declared, that, admitting the necessity of the interference of Government to be apparent, that interference should be such as the Constitution of this country knows, and acknowledges. If the controling power, now enjoyed by his Majesty's Ministers, is not sufficient, or if the affairs of India are of such a magnitude as to require a new establishment, let there be appointed a third Secretary of State; but let the patronage of the Company remain with the Directors and Proprietors. I contend, said his Lordship, that if we touch that, we seize their property. Let this office be established, as it ought to be, under the Crown. This country can know no other executive power but that of the Crown. I hold this to be the first principle of our Constitution; and when we establish any other power in the kingdom, we destroy the Constitution. There is another point, my Lords, in which I differ most materially — The friends of this bill contend, that the Government of India should be in this country. It is impossible, my Lords; you must govern India, in India; and from the moment a contrary system is adopted, the loss of India will not be very distant. Do we not all know, my Lords, that the powers of men's minds have been called forth in India, in a very wonderful manner, by the unexpected events which have transpired in that country: but the moment you

you deprive the Government upon the spot from discovering and rewarding merit — the moment you fill up all offices in that country from this, those great efforts of the human mind, which have been exerted to our admiration and surprise, will appear no longer. Shall Mr. Hastings, or any other Governor General who may succeed him, be the judge of merit under his own eye; or seven men, at the distance of twelve thousand miles from the seat of action. With respect to the state of the Company's affairs, one of the reasons assigned for the present bill—I think it prosperous, all circumstances considered; nor do I see how the seven new Directors can fill their Treasury any more than the twenty-four gentlemen who are to be removed. As to the mismanagement of the Company's affairs abroad, that, my Lords, is a wide field.

I profess myself an admirer, a great admirer of Mr. Hastings; but, my Lords, I am not so enthusiastic an admirer of that
gentle-

gentleman as to suppose, that, in the twelve years of his government, there are no parts of his conduct not reprehensible. Not that, my Lords, I will say, and with confidence, if that great man had been removed during the war, we should not now be disputing as to the mode by which we should govern India, because, my Lords, we should not have had India to govern. The noble Earl (Sandwich) has given your Lordships a long account of enormities committed in India, but he has totally omitted to state to your Lordships, the dates of the several transactions he has mentioned. He tells you, my Lords, that Mr. Hastings, whose name, by the by, the noble Lord did not mention, though he professed to have a high opinion of him; but he tells you, my Lords, that Mr. Hastings appointed an old woman to be the guardian of the person of the Nabob of Bengal, during his minority; and this is represented as a strange act of absurdity, or something worse. But, my Lords, Mr. Hastings assigned good and sufficient

reasons

reasons for his choice. If a native of rank had been appointed, Mr. Hastings dreaded the influence it would give him in Bengal. If a near male relation, he feared for the Nabob's life. The Directors very warmly approved the choice, and the transaction happened in 1772. Whenever your Lordships go into the whole of Mr. Hastings's conduct, you will find those parts which now appear reprehensible, very different from what they are represented. I speak with respect of the transactions in another place; but surely your Lordships must allow, that the reports of the Select Committee carry upon the very face of them the strongest marks of partiality. To criminate Mr. Hastings, appears the sole end of each report; but, my Lords, has his conduct been fairly represented? I wish, on some future day, to see him at that bar, when I am sure he will recover from your Lordships a complete acquittal from all the charges not brought, but insinuated against him. Look, my Lords, to the great actions of Mr. Hastings, and those who served

ved under him. My Lords, the campaign in Guzzerat, the capture of Ahmedabad and Baſſeen, the ſtorm of Sindia's camp, and the other important events which have occurred during the Maratta war, when the officer of Mr. Haſtings's choice, General Goddard, commanded the Britiſh army, will adorn the page of hiſtory in future times. The ſeparate army formed by Mr. Haſtings to attack the dominions of Madajee Scindia; the capture of the important, and, till then, impregnable fortreſs of Gualior, by Colonel Popham, is an event worthy to be recorded to the lateſt times. My Lords, it is abſurd, it is ridiculous to ſay Mr. Haſtings was the author of the Maratta war. It began at Bombay: It was concluded in Bengal. The peace was diſapproved of at home. Mr. Haſtings was inſtructed to ſeize the fitteſt opportunity for breaking the treaty. The noble Earl in the green ribband has ſaid Mr. Haſtings called the Maratta war his war. No, my Lords, he never did; but he conjured Mr. Francis and Mr. Wheeler,

as

as they threw the responsibility upon him, from a particular period, to permit him to conduct it, and the merit of the peace is all his own. The merit of relieving the Carnatic, to which we owe the preservation of India, is all his own. Sir Eyre Coote has confessed it. The merit of inducing the Nizam to remain neuter, and of purchasing the march of Colonel Pearse's army through the Maratta country, is all his own. The time will come, when these services will be acknowledged. When your Lordships shall make the insurrection of Benares, or the state of the Vizier's country the subject of enquiry, Mr. Hastings's conduct will then appear in a very different point of view; allowances will be made for the difficulties with which the State was surrounded. We were the sovereigns of Benares, and Mr. Hastings had a right to exact military service from the Zemindar. Do your Lordships mean, that under no circumstances military service is to be exacted? If so, your empire in India may be short indeed.' On such a tenure, no Zemindar in India ever stood. It is in proof, from the evidence of Captain Harper, to the Select Committee, that Bulwant Sing, father of Cheyt Sing, always furnished his quota of military force to his Sovereign in time of war, independent of the annual revenue he paid—we became the Sovereign—we had a right to exact military service, and it was strictly consonant to the constitution of the Mogul empire. My Lords, if I view Mr. Hastings as a financier, how much reason shall I have to admire his conduct? When he arrived in Bengal in 1772, the Company owed upon bond, one million three hundred thousand pounds: this debt he paid off. I respect the memories of the gentlemen who were sent to India in 1774, and died there; but unfortunate was it indeed for this country, that they so very early differed from Mr. Hastings, and carried their differencies to so great a height—If they had not, Bengal would have been the first Government in the world. Can there, my Lords, be a greater proof of Mr. Hastings's tings's knowledge of the revenues of Bengal than this? That he has actually increased them one million sterling, and preserved his own provinces in tranquillity, though war has desolated other parts of India. — Let not your Lordships be carried away by idle declamation — examine into facts, and you will find that Bengal is in a flourishing situation; and that, perhaps, no country has improved so much as that has done, since Mr. Hastings governed it, though he came there only two years after a destructive famine, which had swept away above a third of the inhabitants of Bengal. Peace is now completely restored — retrenchments in expence have taken place in every department; and in a very few years our situation in India will be more flourishing than ever, if we do not ruin that country by the measures adopted in this. I know no man but Mr. Hastings who can reduce your expences, and pay off your debts in India. He will do it, I am confident, if he is properly and constantly supported from home; and therefore I cannot approve a bill, which has for its object the removal and disgrace of so great a man, were my other objections, which are invincible, done away.

The Earl of Derby followed, and supported the bill upon the necessity there was for checking the public delinquency of the servants of the Company in India. He adduced a variety of letters and extracts to prove the barbarity that had been exercised in that country; then went into the transactions of Mr. Hastings with Cheyt Sing, whose conduct he highly reprobated, both for cruelty and breach of public faith to that prince; and after dwelling for a considerable time on the different proceedings of the Councils of Bengal, Madras, and Bombay, all of whom he charged with a variety of delinquency at different periods, from 1763, he concluded with saying, that he saw how the bill was to go; and it was an appearance which in his mind was most alarming to the independence of Parliament; for without referring to any particular

lar rumour, and without mentioning or alluding to the name of any Peer, he must say that the circumstances attending that bill shewed, that there had been an interference of a most unconstitutional kind. What else could there have been, when they saw that after members had pledged themselves in the most sacred and unequivocal manner to the support of this bill, they should now change their opinion and act against it? To what could such conduct be assigned, but an interference which their Lordships ought to dread more than any calamity that could be derived from the operation of this bill, admitting even that its operation should be as calamitous as it was stated to be. Better that the territories of India should for ever be lost to this country, than that an interposition should exist by which the independence of this House should be destroyed.

Lord Camden said, that he came down unsolicited, and unconnected, to deliver his candid and independent opinion on the bill.

bill. He declared himself an enemy to its principle, for it was a moſt violent infringement of the property of the greateſt Company in the world. It in fact deprives them of their property; for though under the bill, there was a ſpecious appearance of the property being preſerved for the benefit of the Company, yet, when it was conſidered that that property was to be put in truſt; that it was to be managed by others; and that thoſe who were to manage it, were neither to be appointed nor controled by the Proprietors, their Lordſhips would believe that it was in fact a deprivation of property: for if a ſteward, or truſtee was placed in the poſſeſſion of their Lordſhips' rents and rights, and that ſteward or truſtee was neither to be dependent on, nor to be controled by them, would they imagine that they had any available property in their eſtates? It was the quality of property to be ſubject only to the owner. It changed its nature when he loſt his authority over it. A perſon who had delivered his property over to the management of another in truſt,

might,

might, indeed, have a certain annual benefit from it, but he was not the independent possessor of his own property, for he could not convert it to his own uses, nor take any advantage from it, but his annual stipend.

This bill, therefore, pronounced either a commission of bankruptcy, or of lunacy on the Company. It pronounced them to be either unable, from want of property, to proceed in their trade, or from want of mental capacity. The only argument for this violent measure was, that of necessity; a plea which had been used by every Minister, good and bad, and also by every King for the worst and most atrocious acts that were ever perpetrated. Necessity was one of those vague terms which might always be used with or without meaning; but in this case nothing could be admitted as an argument, but a great State necessity. Did such a necessity exist? He believed not; or at least it did not appear on the face of their proceedings, or on any

of

of the grounds which had been exhibited. The Company were not proved to be in a bankrupt ſtate. They had produced a ſtatement of their finances. They had ſhewn that by the calamities of war they had ſuffered a loſs of ſeveral millions, in conſequence of exertions which operated to the advantage of this country. They had ſhewn that their embarraſſments were merely temporary; their creditors were not clamorous; their circumſtances were not deſperate. Nothing was more common in the contingencies of a merchant's fortune, than that in a hard run upon his credit, he ſhould call together his friends, expoſe his circumſtances, and when his creditors found that his bottom was good, to give him time, and rank him in the ſame ſolid eſtimation as before. This was exactly the Company's caſe. They wanted nothing but indulgence for a ſhort time; they expoſed their books to Government for the purpoſe of convincing them that their credit was good; aud no neceſſity appeared that juſtified the violent infringement attempted by this bill.

Did

Did there a necessity exist of another kind? Were the present conductors of the Company's affairs incapable of managing them? He said, they were not proved by any evidence that he had seen to be incapable. Nothing had even been imputed of blame to the Court of Directors. They were acknowledged to have written their dispatches with the most sensible policy; and to have studied, pursued, and accomplished the real interests of the Company. But certain abuses were mentioned, and the conduct of Mr. Hastings was brought forward, to prove how shamefully the affairs of the Company had been administered in India. Without entering into the question of Mr. Hastings, who was, by the bye, the soul of our success in India, he asked, if, when Government interfered, they had been able to punish guilt more than the Court of Directors? He instanced the case of the persons convicted for the treatment of Lord Pigot. When those men came into the court to receive judgment, they came with their pocket books full of bank notes, and proposed with as much

much facility to pay 20,000l. as they paid 1000l. Was this the inftance by which the officers in India were to be taught, that they were not to commit crimes with impunity? It was idle to talk of the guilt of the Court of Directors in fuch inftances as thefe, when Government had, in fact, given their countenance to every meafure of the Directors for many years paft. Give the Court of Directors the power that is given by this bill to the feven new Directors, and try if then they will not be able to regulate the affairs of the Company in India. Free them from the controul of the Proprietary, and fubject their difpatches to the perufal of Minifters, and you will not be oppofed by all men, as acting the part of violators and deftroyers of rights fecured by charters. In no part of this whole bufinefs did there appear any other neceffity for the bill, but the neceffity that Minifters muft keep their places. This was the only neceffity which appeared; and that that was the only neceffity which had given rife to the bill, appeared from one claufe of it — that which gave the Minifter the power of appointing to

every

every office in India, great and small. The influence of the Crown had been curtailed by certain bills, and they required this bill to supply the place of those acts which diminished the influence — and, indeed, it did it in a most ample manner. He called the House to remember what pains, what efforts they had used to gain those points; and were they now to pass a bill which granted more patronage than was possessed by almost any potentate in Europe? He spoke of the Marquis of Rocking's steady perseverance to the end in the doctrines of Whiggism, and lamented that some of those who called themselves his friends, should now favour a system so inimical to that system which it had been the labour and end of that great man's life to establish.

Earl Fitzwilliam entered at considerable length into the arguments for the bill, and to shew that the Company's finances were indeed such as to call for the immediate interference of Parliament; he enumerated a variety of objections to the statement of their

their affairs, pointing out the fallacies of their account, and shewing that they were not only in great and urgent necessities, but that, without the present interposition, they must be precipitated to ruin. He referred to what the noble Lord had said of the principles and purity of the Marquis of Rockingham. He paid him the warmest compliments. Yes, that noble Lord was always against the unnecessary and corrupt influence of the Crown. He had constantly been for the diminution of the power of corruption; but was he an enemy to stable and permanent government? No as he wished for order, for regulation, for peace, and all the comforts of a government soundly administered, he wished to see Administration supported by fair, public, and responsible influence. If that noble Marquis had perceived the sort of influence which was now but too apparent, he would have condemned it with more energy, with more determination, and considered it with more alarm than he could express in words. His mind, filled and actuated by the motives of Whiggism, would ill brook to see a dark and secret influence

fluence exerting itself against the independence of Parliament, and the authority of Ministers.

Lord King spoke against the bill, and with considerable heat demanded, if, as it was said, that certain Peers were influenced by secret and unavowed means, he was ranked among the number. He dared any man to say that he was dictated to in his opinion on this or upon any other occasion.

Lord Gage supported the bill on the same independent ground. He had connections with no Ministers. He had received favours from none since the days of his friend the Duke of Newcastle.

The Earl of Radnor opposed the bill as a most violent infringement on the liberties of the Company, and, with theirs, on the liberties of the people.

The Bishop of Salisbury said, that if Ministers would say that in the Committee, some clauses to which he objected would be expunged, he would vote for the commitment.

mitment. He mentioned what those clauses were. He thought the principle of the bill a good one.

The Earl of Carlisle said, that on the question of commitment it was impossible to say what the Committee would do.

The Earl of Coventry then moved, that the bill be rejected.

Some conversation occurred on an expression thrown out by Earl Fitzwilliam in the preceding debate, which being satisfactorily explained, the question was put, and the bill rejected without a second division.

The following is an accurate LIST of the Division in the House of LORDS on Monday last; and also of the Division on Wednesday:

MONDAY, December 15.

HOUSE of LORDS on the INDIA BILL, it was moved to adjourn.

CONTENTS.

Abps. Canterbury	Dukes of Richmond	Dukes of Brandon
York	Rutland	Chandos
		Dukes

[151]

Dukes of Dorset
Bridgewater
Earls of Salisbury
Denbigh
Winchelsea
Chesterfield
Essex
Doncaster
Abingdon
Coventry
Galloway
Aberdeen
Dunmore
Marchmont
Ferrers
Tankerville
Aylsford
Harborough
Macclesfield
Effingham
Brooke ———
Gower
Temple
Harcourt
Cornwallis
Delawar
Radnor
Chatham

Earl of Clarendon
Bathurst
Ailesbury
Vis. Weymouth
Sackville
Bishops of Salisbury
Rochester
Worcester
Chester
Exeter
Lincoln
Litchfield and Coventry
Lords Abergavenny
De Ferrars
Percy
Paget
St. John
Osborne
Romney
King
Talbot
Chedworth
Vere
Grantham
Scarsdale
Boston
Beaulieu

Lords Walsingham
Camden
Amherst
Thurlow
Brudenell
Grantley
Rawdon
Sydney   6
BY PROXY.
Duke of Leeds
Queensberry
Northumberland
Marquis of Lothian
Earls of Pembroke
Stanhope
Waldegrave
Darlington
Hillsborough
Visc. Wentworth
Courtenay
Bishops of London
Durham
Bangor
Lords Say and Sele
Middleton
Fortescue
Hawke   13

NOT CONTENTS.

Prince of Wales
Dukes of Devonshire
Portland
Manchester
Earls of Derby
Suffolk
Westmoreland
Peterborough
Stamford
Sandwich
Carlisle
Plymouth
Scarborough
Jersey
Cholmondeley
Glencairn
Cassilis

Earls of Powis
Lauderdale
Dartmouth
Buckinghamshire
Fitzwilliam
Egremont
Ilchester
Spencer
Mansfield
Viscounts Hereford
Townshend
Stormont
Maynard
Hampden
Keppel
Bp. of Winchester
Peterborough

Bp. of Oxford
St. David's
Gloucester
Bristol
Lords Audley
Craven
Boyle
Cadogan
Monson
Montfort
Sandys
Ponsonby
Walpole
Sondes
Pelham
Vernon
Cardiff

Lords

Lords Brownlow   Duke of Atholl   Earl of Northington
  Harrowby   Earls of Exeter   Viscount Leinster
  Foley   Oxford   Bishops of Carlisle
  Loughborough   Eglingtoun   Norwich
  Gage   Roseberry   Lords Willoughby
  Bagot   57   Sussex   Teynham
  By Proxy.   Harrington   Onslow
Dukes of Bolton   Guildford   Rivers
  Marlborough   Hardwicke   Bagot
  Gordon   Fauconberg. ✓   22

CONTENTS,

Peers ——— — 75
Proxies ——— — 20
                    ——— 95

NOT CONTENTS.

Peers ——— — 57
Proxies ——— — 19
                    ——— 76
                    ———
                        79

WEDNESDAY, December 17.
That the said BILL be rejected.

CONTENTS.

As before   69 Earl of Mansfield   PROXIES.
  Deduct   Viscount Stormont   As before   18
Bp. of Rochester 1   Howe   Add
                 —   Lord Grosvenor   Earl of Oxford
                 68   Milton   Lord Dacre
  Add   2
Duke of Ancaster   7
Earl of Abercorn   ———   ———
                                        75   20

NOT CONTENTS.

As before   57   Add   PROXIES.
  Deduct   Earl of Huntingdon As before   22
Prince of Wales   Hertford   Deduct
Earl of Egmont   Viscount Montagu   Earl of Oxford
  Mansfield   Lord Stawell   Hardwick
Viscount Stormont   4 Lord Rivers   3
                 4   ———   ———
                ———   57
                 53

www.ingramcontent.com/pod-product-compliance
Lightning Source LLC
Chambersburg PA
CBHW030320170426
43202CB00009B/1077